PIONEER

American edition

beginners

H. Q. Mitchell – Marileni Malkogianni

student's book

mm
publications

PIONEER BEGINNERS CONTENTS

Reading	Listening	Speaking (Pronunciation/Intonation*)	Writing
• A comic strip: *Teacher trouble...*	• People greeting, introducing others and saying goodbye • Short formal and informal dialogues discussing personal information • A formal conversation requesting personal information	• Pair work: Greeting each other • Group work: Greeting, introducing and saying goodbye • Group work: Talking about jobs • Pair work game: Asking questions to guess the person • Pair work: Exchanging personal information (age, phone number, address, e-mail) • Presenting oneself and others • Pair work: Saying where you're from and where you live • Pair work: Spelling names * Numbers (fifteen vs. fifty)	• Sentences about yourself • Making a business card • Completing a form **Developing skills:** • Capital letters
• A magazine article: *What's your favorite gadget?*	• Three short dialogues about gadgets • A conversation between a woman and an airport official • A conversation about a teacher	• Group work: Asking and answering questions about a family tree • Presenting oneself and family members • Pair work: Expressing opinion about gadgets • Pair work game: Identifying objects • Pair work: Identifying the contents of one's bag • Pair work: Describing people • Pair work game: Guessing the person being described * /s/, /z/, /ɪz/ (plural –s)	• Sentences about yourself and family members • Sentences about your favorite gadget • A paragraph describing a person **Developing skills:** • Punctuation • Capital letters
• A short text: *Pastry Patty* • A magazine interview: *Life as a... Game Tester!*	• Three short dialogues about sports • A street survey about spare time • Three short dialogues about TV shows	• Pair work: Talking about routine • Group work: Talking about sport preferences and making suggestions • Pair work: Talking about spare-time activities • Pair work: Conducting and taking part in a survey about spare time • Group work: Talking about TV shows and preferences * Third-person singular –s * Intonation of questions	• Sentences comparing people's daily routines • A profile for a social media site **Developing skills:** • Word order • Planning and organizing your writing
• A magazine article: *My guide to simple housework* • House advertisements	• A street survey about chores • A conversation about which apartment to rent • Two short dialogues about where one lives	• Pair work: Talking about chores • Group work: Speculating about the location of objects • Pair work: Talking about one's bedroom • Pair work: Discussing which apartment to rent • Pair work: Talking about where you live • Pair work: Describing one's house/apartment * Intonation of questions and answers	• Sentences about one's bedroom • A description of a house / an apartment **Developing skills:** • Aspects of sentence structure • Listing things
• An Internet forum: *How do you get around the city?* • A poster: *Green Neighborhood*	• A radio report about traffic • Three short dialogues discussing directions • Four short dialogues taking place at different places in a city	• Class discussion about getting around • Group survey: *Can you...?* • Pair work: Asking for and giving directions • Class discussion about how "green" one's neighborhood is • Group work: Discussing changes and planning events • Group work: Talking about one's town/city * /ʃ/, /s/, /tʃ/	• A description of one's town/city **Developing skills:** • Avoiding repetition • Planning and organizing your writing

		Vocabulary	Grammar	Functions
6 p.57	Grab a bite	• Food and drink • Food categories • Conversational English • Phrases denoting quantity	• Countable and Uncountable nouns • a(n) / some • some / any • How much...? / How many...?	• Talking about food preferences and eating habits • Asking and answering about quantity • Understanding menus • Ordering food and drink • Making, accepting and refusing offers
		Task: Creating, conducting and reporting the results of a survey		
7 p.67	Online	• Ways of communicating • Telephone language • Conversational English • Computer language • The weather	• Present Progressive	• Talking about current activities • Talking on the phone • Asking for help and offering help • Thanking and responding to thanks • Guessing the meaning of words in context • Discussing facts • Making suggestions • Talking about the weather
		Task: Collaborating and creating a quiz about technology		
8 p.77	Memories	• School subjects • Years • Conversational English • Word building: nouns ending in *-er* and *-or* referring to people • Life events • Parts of the body	• Past Simple • Past Simple of the verb *to be* • There was / There were	• Talking about past events/experiences • Giving reason • Talking about famous people in history and their achievements • Understanding dictionary entries • Talking about accidents and responding to bad news
		Task: Collaborating with others to write a biography		
9 p.87	Extreme	• Numbers over a hundred • Clothes • Sizes • Prices • Words/Phrases related to shopping • Conversational English • Words/Phrases related to space • Animals • Extreme sports	• Comparative forms • Superlative forms	• Making comparisons • Talking about clothes and expressing preference • Talking about prices and sizes • Discussing facts • Expressing opinion, agreement and disagreement • Discussing past experiences
		Task: Collaborating with a partner to reach a decision based on specific criteria		
10 p.97	Get away	• Types of vacation • Seasons • Months • Geographical features • Vacation activities • Conversational English	• Future *going to* • The verb *should*	• Talking about vacations • Talking about dates and seasons • Locating information on tickets, schedules, etc. • Making plans and future arrangements • Inviting, accepting and refusing an invitation • Asking for and giving advice • Expressing opinion and giving reason
		Task: Prioritizing and reaching a decision		

Reading	Listening	Speaking (Pronunciation/Intonation*)	Writing
• A magazine article: *Vegetarian or Meat eater?* • A comic strip: *Mrs. Pickles*	• A conversation between a waiter and a couple ordering • Four people answering questions for a survey • Two short dialogues	• Pair work: Discussing food preferences and eating habits • Pair work: Role play at a restaurant • Group work: Conducting and taking part in a survey • Class discussion about food from other countries • Pair work: Asking for and giving information about a restaurant • Pair work: Talking about people's eating habits in your country * /g/, /dʒ/	• Sentences about food preferences • A short text about eating habits **Developing skills:** • Linking words (and, but, or) • Planning and organizing your writing
• A feature article: *Keyboard shortcuts*	• Two short dialogues • A radio show about a computer quiz • Three short dialogues about the weather	• Pair work: Role play talking on the phone • Pair work: Using guidelines to hold a conversation • Group work: Discussing facts • Class discussion about the weather • Group work: Discussing, making suggestions and deciding what to do • Pair work: An everyday conversation * /n/, /ŋ/ * Word stress	• A quiz • A letter / An e-mail to a friend **Developing skills:** • Set phrases for informal letters/e-mails
• Two short e-mails about a day out • A factual text: *The Brontë Sisters*	• Three short dialogues about school memories • A radio show about a famous person in history • A conversation about an accident	• Pair work: Talking about yesterday • Pair work: Talking about one's school years • Group game: Guessing the famous person in history • Pair work: Discussing an accident * /t/, /d/, /ɪd/	• A short e-mail about the recent past • A short biography • A paragraph about a bad day **Developing skills:** • Linking words/phrases to list events
• A comic strip: *Big Shorts* • Quiz: *Cosmic quiz!* • A webpage: *Help Save Snow Leopards!*	• A science teacher talking to his class • A conversation about mountain gorillas • A conversation at a rock climbing school	• Class discussion about clothes and prices • Group work: Role play at a clothing store • Pair work game: Presenting facts and guessing the planet • Pair work: Discussing what to buy and reaching a decision • Group work: Talking about extreme sports • Pair work: Talking about past experiences * /ɪ/, /iː/	• An e-mail describing an experience **Developing skills:** • Linking words (because, so)
• A booking confirmation, tickets, schedules, etc. showing someone's vacation plans • A webpage: *Advice for travelers going abroad*	• A conversation between a couple while on vacation • Four monologues about what these people can't go camping without • A conversation about a vacation	• Pair work: Using dates • Pair work: Making plans for a trip • Group work: Inviting, accepting and refusing an invitation • Pair work: Discussing what to take on a camping trip • Group work: Matching people with vacations • Pair work: Discussing while on vacation * /θ/, /ð/ * Silent letters	• A short e-mail about vacation plans • An e-mail while on vacation **Developing skills:** • Using appropriate tenses and time expressions

American and British English p.120   *Phonetic Symbols p.121*   *Listening Transcripts p. 122*   *Word list p. 130*

Classroom language ◀))

The Alphabet ◀))

Hello there!

I'm Janet.

Discuss:
- Do you like meeting new people?
- What do you usually talk about?

I'm John.

I'm Mike.

I'm Betty.

My name's Andy. What's your name?

In this module you will learn...

- to greet people and say goodbye in formal and informal situations
- to introduce yourself and others
- to use numbers (0-100)
- to understand information on business cards
- to exchange basic personal information (name, age, job, telephone number, address, e-mail, nationality)
- to say where you're from
- to spell names
- to complete a form

1 Vocabulary ◀))

Listen. What would you say to greet someone right now?

Good morning! → 12:00 P.M. → Good afternoon! → 6:00 P.M. → Good evening!

2 Reading ◀))

A. Listen, read and match the dialogues with the pictures.

a

b

c

d

1

A: Hello?
B: Hi, Maria. How are you?
A: Not bad. And you?
B: I'm OK, thanks.

2

A: Hi, John!
B: Hey, Mark. What's up?
A: Not much. How's it going?
B: Great.

3

A: Good morning, Tom.
B: Hello, Jeff. This is Kevin.
A: Nice to meet you, Kevin.
C: Nice to meet you, too.

4

A: Good afternoon, Mrs. Rogers.
   How are you?
B: Good afternoon, Ms. Langley.
   I'm fine, and you?
A: I'm very well, thank you.

Male: Mr. + last name
Female: Miss / Mrs. / Ms. + last name

B. Read again. Are the dialogues formal or informal?

3 Speaking

Talk in pairs. Greet each other using the phrases given.

> *Good morning,...*
> *Hello,... How are you?*
> *...*

Good morning, etc.	I'm OK/good, thanks.
Hello. How are you?	Great!
Hi. How's it going?	I'm fine. / Fine.
Not bad. And you?	I'm very well, thank you.

4 Vocabulary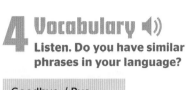

Listen. Do you have similar phrases in your language?

Goodbye. / Bye.
See you.
See you later.
See you tomorrow.
Take care.
Have a nice day.

5 Listening

A. Listen and choose the correct reply.

1. **a.** Good afternoon.
   b. Great!

2. **a.** I'm Steven.
   b. Fine, thanks. And you?

3. **a.** Goodbye!
   b. I'm OK.

4. **a.** Bye! Have a nice day.
   b. Not bad.

5. **a.** I'm OK.
   b. Ryan.

6. **a.** Nice to meet you, too.
   b. See you!

7. **a.** Nice to meet you, too.
   b. Hello, Mary.

8. **a.** Not much.
   b. I'm Tina.

B. Now, listen again and give your own reply.

6 Speaking

Talk in groups of three. Practice greeting, introducing each other and saying goodbye.

> *Hello, Tony.*
> *Hi, Greg! How's it going?*
> *Great, thanks. This is Jack.*
> *Nice to meet you, Jack.*
> *Nice to meet you, too.*
> *OK, see you later.*
> *Bye. Have a nice day.*
> *You too!*

TIP

When doing speaking activities, speak only in English. Don't be afraid to make mistakes.

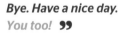

1 Reading 🔊
A. Listen and read. Who is Ken Holmes?

TEACHER TROUBLE...

B. Read again and complete with Jake, Ken or Steve.

1. "I'm a teacher at the college." _____

2. "We're friends." _____ and _____

3. "I'm not a student." _____

4. "My last name's Holmes." _____

> **Most plural nouns take -s.**
> a student → students

2 Vocabulary & Speaking 🔊

A. Listen. Which of the people can you find at a hospital, school or restaurant?

nurse

chef

electrician

architect

police officer

firefighter

bus driver

waiter/waitress

actor/actress

dentist

student

teacher

secretary

doctor

B. Talk in groups.

❝ *What do you do?*
I'm a nurse. What do you do?
I'm an architect. What about you?
I'm unemployed. ❞

a doctor
an electrician

3 Grammar The verb *to be* (I, you, we), Possessive adjectives (my, your, our) → *p. 111*

A. Read the examples and write the short forms in the table.

> I'm a firefighter. I'm not a police officer.
> You're a chef. You aren't a waiter.
> We're nurses. We aren't doctors.
> Are you English? → Yes, I am. / No, I'm not.
> → Yes, we are. / No, we aren't.

FULL FORMS	SHORT FORMS
I am	I'm
You are	_____
We are	_____
are not	_____

B. Complete with *my*, *your* or *our*.

> I'm Debbie.
> _____ last name's Baker.

> We're students.
> This is _____ school.

> Hello.
> What's _____ name?

C. Circle the correct words.

Mike Good morning, I'm Mike and this is Jenny.

Woman Hello. What's your last name?

Mike **Your / Our** last name's Cooper.

Woman Mike and Jenny Cooper. **You are / Are you** an actress, Mrs. Cooper?

Jenny No, I **am not / aren't**. Mike and I **we're / are** architects.

4 Speaking Guessing game
Talk in pairs. Go to page 107.

5 Writing
Write a few sentences about yourself.

> I'm Lisa Smith.
> I'm a student at Highland College.

1 Vocabulary ◀))

**Can you say these numbers?
Listen and check.**

0 zero						
1 one	6 six	11 eleven	16 sixteen	21 twenty-one	26 twenty-six	40 forty
2 two	7 seven	12 twelve	17 seventeen	22 twenty-two	27 twenty-seven	50 fifty
3 three	8 eight	13 thirteen	18 eighteen	23 twenty-three	28 twenty-eight	60 sixty
4 four	9 nine	14 fourteen	19 nineteen	24 twenty-four	29 twenty-nine	70 seventy
5 five	10 ten	15 fifteen	20 twenty	25 twenty-five	30 thirty	80 eighty
						90 ninety
						100 one hundred

2 Pronunciation ◀))

A. Listen and repeat. Notice the difference in pronunciation.

fif**teen** - **fif**ty   thir**teen** - **thir**ty

B. Listen and check the correct number.

1. 16 ☐   60 ☐
2. 18 ☐   80 ☐
3. 17 ☐   70 ☐
4. 14 ☐   40 ☐
5. 19 ☐   90 ☐

3 Speaking

A. Look at the following. What are they? Match.

335-679-2290

9670 Park Road

44 years old

franky200@intermail.com

age

e-mail address

address

phone number

B. Talk in pairs. Read the note and exchange personal information.

❝ *How old are you?*
    I'm ... (years old).
What's your cell phone number / home number?
    ...
What's your address / e-mail address?
    ... ❞

> **phone number:** 435-876-8910 =
> four-three-five, eight-seven-six, eight-nine-one-zero
> **address:** 175 White Street =
> number + name of Street/Road/Avenue
> **e-mail:** dianastone3@gmail.com =
> Diana Stone 3 'at' gmail 'dot' com

4 Reading ◀))

A. Listen and read.

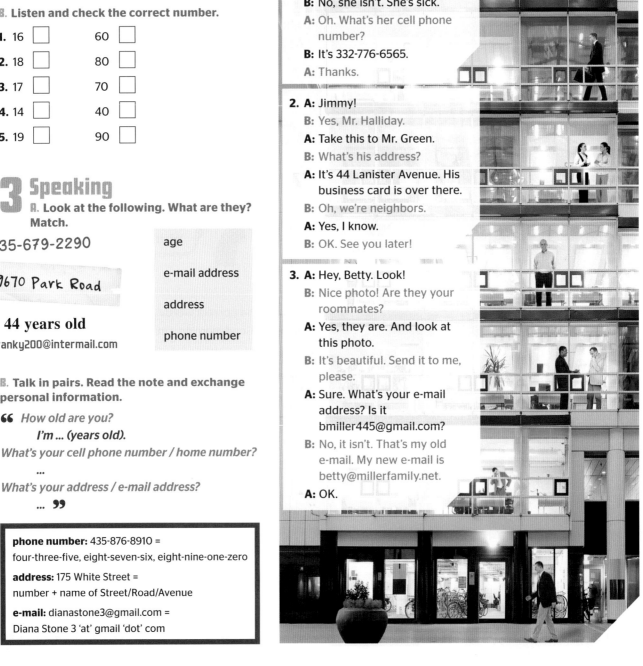

1. **A:** Is Josie here today?
   B: No, she isn't. She's sick.
   A: Oh. What's her cell phone number?
   B: It's 332-776-6565.
   A: Thanks.

2. **A:** Jimmy!
   B: Yes, Mr. Halliday.
   A: Take this to Mr. Green.
   B: What's his address?
   A: It's 44 Lanister Avenue. His business card is over there.
   B: Oh, we're neighbors.
   A: Yes, I know.
   B: OK. See you later!

3. **A:** Hey, Betty. Look!
   B: Nice photo! Are they your roommates?
   A: Yes, they are. And look at this photo.
   B: It's beautiful. Send it to me, please.
   A: Sure. What's your e-mail address? Is it bmiller445@gmail.com?
   B: No, it isn't. That's my old e-mail. My new e-mail is betty@millerfamily.net.
   A: OK.

B. Read again and write the correct names.

1. "My address is 44 Lanister Avenue." _____

2. "Mr. Green and I are neighbors." _____

3. "My cell phone number is 332-776-6565." _____

4. "My old e-mail address is bmiller445@gmail.com."

_____

5. "I'm sick today." _____

5 Grammar The verb *to be* (he, she, it, they), Possessive adjectives (his, her, their)
→ *p. 111*

A. Read the examples and write the short forms in the table.

> Jack's my best friend.
> **He's** 15 years old. **He isn't** 17.
>
> Lucy is my roommate.
> **She's** at home today. **She isn't** at school.
>
> This is my cell phone.
> **It's** new. **It isn't** old.
>
> Is he/she/it nice? → **Yes, he/she/it is.**
> → **No, he/she/it isn't.**
>
> **They're** neighbors. **They aren't** roommates.
>
> Are they friends? → **Yes, they are.**
> → **No, they aren't.**

FULL FORMS	SHORT FORMS
He is	_____
She is	_____
It is	_____
They are	_____
is not	_____
are not	_____

B. Match. When do we use the words in blue?

He's a doctor.   **Her** phone number is 555-613-8091.

She's my best friend.   **Their** restaurant is on Field Road.

They're chefs.   **His** name is Dr. Myers.

C. Circle the correct words.

1. **A:** Jack and Bill **is / are** best friends.

   B: They are / Are they roommates, too?

   A: No, they **isn't / aren't**. **They're / Their** neighbors.

   B: What do they do? **Is / Are** Jack a police officer?

   A: No. He **is / isn't** a firefighter.

   B: What about Bill?

   A: His / He's unemployed.

2. **A:** Look! There's Nora and **her / their** roommate.

   B: What's **his / her** name?

   A: Amy.

   B: Is she / She is a student, too?

   A: No, she **isn't / aren't**. **She's / She** a waitress.

A. Which of the information below do you think should be on a business card?

> name   address   age   e-mail
> phone number   job

B. Listen. Match the dialogues with the business cards. Write 1-3. There is one extra business card that you will not need to use.

Emma Osbourne
architect

a ☐

Tel.: 112-335-1100
eosbourne99@hotmail.com
office: 87 Billbury Avenue, Downsville

b ☐

ROGER BLACKBURN
electrician
home 334-556-5546
cell 999-501-6723
rblackburn556@gmail.com

Ryan Black dentist

Phone: 112-443-9987
ryan@blackdent.com
office: 334 Clifton Street, Morecroft

c ☐

Emily Orwell
nurse

d ☐

199-443-4545
emilyorwell22@gmail.com

C. Talk about the people in the business cards.

❝ *Her name is...*
She's a/an...
Her e-mail is... ❞

D. Talk in pairs.

Student A: Imagine you are a graphic designer. Ask Student B questions to get the information you need to make a business card for him/her.

❝ *What's your name?*
What do you do?
What's your...? ❞

Student B: Imagine you need a business card. Answer the graphic designer's (Student A's) questions.

E. Give out your business card to other classmates and introduce yourself.

❝ *Hi, I'm Nigel Winters. I'm a chef at...* ❞

1d

1 Vocabulary & Speaking 🔊

A. Match. Then listen and check your answers.

COUNTRIES	NATIONALITIES
Argentina	Italian
Australia	Brazilian
Brazil	Russian
Canada	Polish
China	Peruvian
Egypt	Australian
France	Irish
Hungary	Canadian
Ireland	Chinese
Italy	American
Mexico	Argentinian/ Argentine
Peru	
Poland	Turkish
Russia	British
Spain	Hungarian
the U.K.	Spanish
the U.S.A.	Mexican
Turkey	French
	Egyptian

- the U.S.A. = the United States of America (the U.S., the States)
- the U.K. = the United Kingdom of Great Britain and Northern Ireland

B. Talk in pairs.

66 *Where are you from?*
I'm from... but/and I live in... And you? 99

in + city/country
I live in London.

Practice the spelling and pronunciation of new words. **TIP**

2 Speaking & Listening 🔊

A. Talk in pairs.

66 *What's your first name?*
Lisa.
What's your last name?
Thomson.
How do you spell your last name?
It's T-H-O-M-S-O-N. 99

B. Listen to part of a conversation between a woman and a man. What is the man's name?

a. John Davis.
b. Jon Davies.
c. Jon Davis.

C. Listen to the rest of the conversation. Find four mistakes in the application form below and correct them.

APPLICATION FORM

TITLE: Mr. ☑ - Mrs. ☐ - Miss ☐ - Ms. ☐

FIRST NAME(S): _____
LAST NAME: D_____
AGE: 34
NATIONALITY: Australian
OCCUPATION: dentist

HOME NUMBER: 221 - 554 - 8898
CELL PHONE NUMBER: 245 - 575 - 5998
E-MAIL: jd445@gmail.com

3 Writing Complete a form

A. Read the note and add capitals to the sentences 1-7.

Capital letters

Use capital letters:
- with first and last names
- with Mr./Mrs./Miss/Ms./Dr.
- with streets/roads/avenues, etc.
- with cities/countries/ nationalities

1. How are you, julian?
2. My name is george ingles.
3. Are you spanish?
4. Is freddie your roommate?
5. lucy isn't canadian. She's from france.
6. This is mr. king.
7. My address is 905 walkley street.

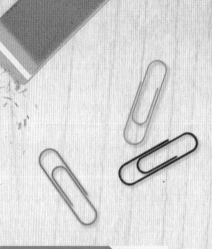

B. Complete the form.

TIP

When completing a form, make sure you understand what information you are asked to give.

APPLICATION FORM

TITLE: Mr. ☐ - Mrs. ☐ - Miss ☐ - Ms. ☐

FIRST NAME: _____

LAST NAME: _____

AGE: _____

NATIONALITY: _____

OCCUPATION: _____

HOME NUMBER: _____

CELL PHONE NUMBER: _____

E-MAIL: _____

ADDRESS: _____

I, _____, certify that the information given on this form is, to the best of my knowledge, correct and complete.

Signature_____ Date_____

4 Speaking

Look at the form above with your information and present yourself to your partner or to the class. It's up to you what information to give and what to leave out.

Vocabulary

A. Cross out the odd word. Then add one more.

1. sixty – age – twelve – one - _____
2. waitress – dentist – neighbor – bus driver - _____
3. Egypt – Irish – American – Chinese - _____
4. Peru – Russia – Spain – French - _____
5. classmate – hospital – office – restaurant - _____

B. Complete with the words in the box.

| care   spell   sick   unemployed   business   live |

1. Greg isn't at school today. He's at home. He's _____.
2. Here's my _____ card. I'm an electrician.
3. I'm from Canada but I _____ in New York.
4. How do you _____ your first name?
5. **A:** Is Tony a waiter?
   B: No, he's _____.
6. **A:** Have a nice day!
   B: You too. Take _____.

Grammar

C. Choose a, b or c.

1. Charlie's a dentist. ____ phone number is 678-900-8732.
   a. He   **b.** He's   **c.** His
2. Are you ____ actress?
   a. a   **b.** an   **c.** –
3. **A:** Are you Katie Williams?
   B: I'm Katie but ____ last name isn't Williams.
   a. your   **b.** my   **c.** her
4. Kelly and Tina are ____ doctors.
   a. a   **b.** an   **c.** –
5. **A:** Lee and Kim are from China.
   B: Really? What's ____ last name?
   A: Wong.
   a. their   **b.** your   **c.** our
6. This is Lucy and ____ classmate Maria.
   a. her   **b.** his   **c.** she's

D. Circle the correct words.

1. We **isn't / aren't** from Argentina. We **is / are** from Brazil.
2. **A: Is / Are** your neighbors Spanish?
   B: Yes, **we / they** are.
3. **What / What's** is your e-mail?
4. **A: Is / Are** Brian your best friend?
   B: Well, he **is / are** my roommate but he **isn't / aren't** my best friend.
5. **A:** How **am / are** you?
   B: You're / I'm fine.
6. Where **he is / is he** from?

Communication

E. Complete the conversations.

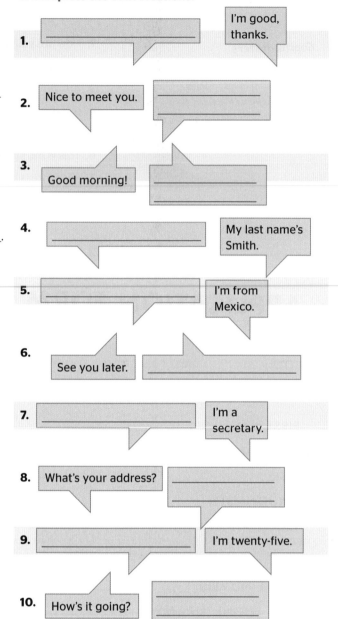

1. _____   I'm good, thanks.

2. Nice to meet you.   _____

3. Good morning!   _____ _____

4. _____   My last name's Smith.

5. _____   I'm from Mexico.

6. See you later.   _____

7. _____   I'm a secretary.

8. What's your address?   _____ _____

9. _____   I'm twenty-five.

10. How's it going?   _____ _____

Self-assessment

Read the following and check the appropriate boxes. For the points you are unsure of, refer back to the relevant sections in the module.

NOW I CAN...

- greet people and say goodbye ☐
- introduce myself and others ☐
- use numbers (0-100) ☐
- understand information on business cards ☐
- exchange basic personal information (name, age, job, telephone number, address, e-mail, nationality) ☐
- say where I'm from ☐
- spell names ☐
- complete a form ☐

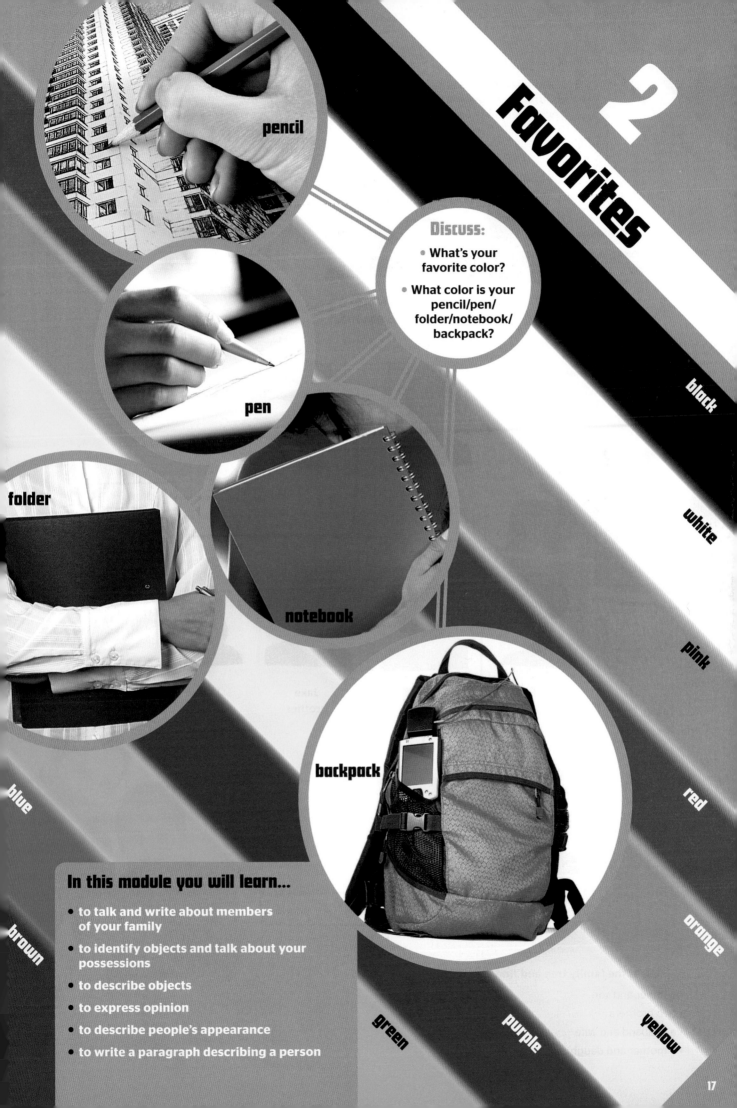

pencil

Discuss:
- What's your favorite color?
- What color is your pencil/pen/folder/notebook/backpack?

pen

folder

notebook

backpack

black

white

pink

red

orange

blue

brown

green

purple

yellow

In this module you will learn...

- to talk and write about members of your family
- to identify objects and talk about your possessions
- to describe objects
- to express opinion
- to describe people's appearance
- to write a paragraph describing a person

2a

1 Vocabulary 🔊

A. Complete Mark's family tree with the words:
children/kids, grandparents, mother/mom.
Then listen and check your answers.

man / boy
woman / girl

Derek
grandfather

Wendy
grandmother

_____

Peter
father/dad

Elsie

_____ parents

Molly
wife

Mark

Jake
brother

Louise
sister

Andy
son

Julie
daughter

_____

B. Look at the family tree and find:

• a father and son
• two brothers
• a husband and wife
• a mother and daughter

18

2 Reading 🔊

A. Look at the pictures. What do you think the people are talking about? Listen, read and find out.

1

Brian	Are you single, Scott?
Scott	No, I'm married and I have two children, a son and a baby daughter.
Brian	And who is this?
Scott	My son, Jason.
Brian	How old is he?
Scott	He's 7.
Brian	My sister has a son. His name is Jason, too, but he's 34.

2

Eddie	Do you have any brothers or sisters?
Rick	Yes, I have two brothers and two sisters. I have a big family.
Eddie	Really? That's nice.
Rick	What about you?
Eddie	I'm an only child.

3

Alison	What's your full name, again?
Linda	It's Linda Summer Barton.
Alison	Summer?
Linda	Yeah. It's my middle name. It's not that bad. My sister's name is Janet Seven Barton.
Alison	Seven? That isn't a name, that's a number!
Linda	Tell my parents.

B. Read again and write T for True or F for False.

1. Scott only has a son. ☐
2. Brian has a sister. ☐
3. Brian is 34. ☐
4. Rick has one sister. ☐
5. Eddie has no brothers or sisters. ☐
6. Linda's middle name is Summer. ☐
7. Alison and Janet are sisters. ☐

3 Grammar — The verb *to have* (affirmative), Possessive case → p. 111

A. Read the examples. What do you notice about the formation of the verb *to have* in the affirmative?

> I **have** a baby sister.
> He / She / It **has** two names.
> We / You / They **have** new cell phones.

B. Read the dialogue. Who has a black folder? Who has a blue folder?

> **Greg** Mary, is this Tony**'s** folder?
> **Mary** No, it isn't. His folder is black. That blue folder is my brother**'s**.

C. Circle the correct words.

1. My brother **has / have** a son and a daughter. His **son / son's** name is Barry and his **daughter / daughter's** name is Nancy.

2. Who's Mrs. Stevens? Is she our new **neighbor / neighbor's**?

3. I **have / has** two best **friends / friend's**. What about you?

4. We **have / has** a new English teacher.

5. **A:** Is this your **notebook / notebook's**?
   B: No, it's **Jane / Jane's**. Jane **have / has** nice notebooks.

D. Talk in groups of four. Look at the family tree in activity 1A and ask and answer questions about the people.

> 66 *Who's Peter?*
> ***Peter is Elsie's husband.***
> *Peter is Jake's father.*
> *Peter is Wendy's son.* 99

4 Speaking & Writing

A. Present yourself and different members of your family to the class.

> 66 *I have a small/big family.*
> *I have...*
> *My brother's/sister's/ etc. name is...*
> *He/She is a/an...*
> *I'm married. My wife's/husband's name is...*
> *He/She is...* 99

B. Write sentences about yourself and your family.

2b

1 Vocabulary 🔊

Match. Then listen and check your answers. Which of the following do you have?

| laptop ☐ | MP4 player ☐ | CDs/DVDs ☐ | headphones ☐ | camera ☐ |
| smartphone ☐ | tablet ☐ | PC (personal computer) ☐ | keyboard ☐ | USB memory stick ☐ |

2 Reading 🔊

A. Look at the pictures and the title of the text. What do you think the people are saying about their gadgets? Listen, read and find out.

What's your favorite gadget?

Tina: My tablet! I have it with me day and night. It has games, books and of course, the Internet. I think it's awesome.

Leo: My MP4 player! I have about 3,000 songs on it. I love music. I also have movies on it, but it has a very small screen.

Barbara: My laptop! It's old, but I like it. New laptops are expensive. I have it with me all the time - at home, at the office and on the train to work.

Tony: My new smartphone! It has a great camera, 12 megapixels. I have lots of pictures of my friends and family on my phone.

B. Read again and write T for True or F for False.

1. Tina's tablet has games on it. ☐
2. Barbara has a new laptop. ☐
3. Barbara has her laptop at work, too. ☐
4. Leo's favorite gadget has a small screen. ☐
5. Tony's favorite gadget is his camera. ☐
6. Tony has pictures only of his friends on his smartphone. ☐

3 Vocabulary

Find opposites for the adjectives below in the text in activity 2.

1. terrible ≠ _____, _____

2. big ≠ _____

3. new ≠ _____

4. cheap ≠ _____

4 Grammar Adjectives → *p. 111*

A. The words in blue are adjectives. What do you notice about their form and position?

> Your phone is **cool**.   You have a **cool** phone.
>
> Lee's headphones are **old**.   Lee has **old** headphones.

B. Complete the second sentence so that it has the same meaning as the first sentence.

1. a. Sandra's MP4 player is new.

   b. Sandra has a _____.

2. a. We have a red camera.

   b. Our camera _____.

3. a. Tom's gadgets are expensive.

   b. Tom has _____.

4. a. I have nice pictures.

   b. My pictures _____.

5. a. This is an awesome CD.

   b. This CD _____.

5 Listening ◀))

Listen to three short dialogues and choose a or b.

1. Roy has a _____ phone.

   a. white   **b.** black

2. Wendy's tablet is _____.

   a. new   **b.** old

3. The laptop is _____.

   a. cheap   **b.** expensive

6 Speaking

Talk in pairs. Go to page 109.

7 Writing

Write a few sentences about one of your favorite gadgets.

> My favorite gadget is my cell phone. I have it with me all the time. It's small and it has_

1 Vocabulary ◀))

Listen. Which of the items in the picture do you think people usually have in their bags?

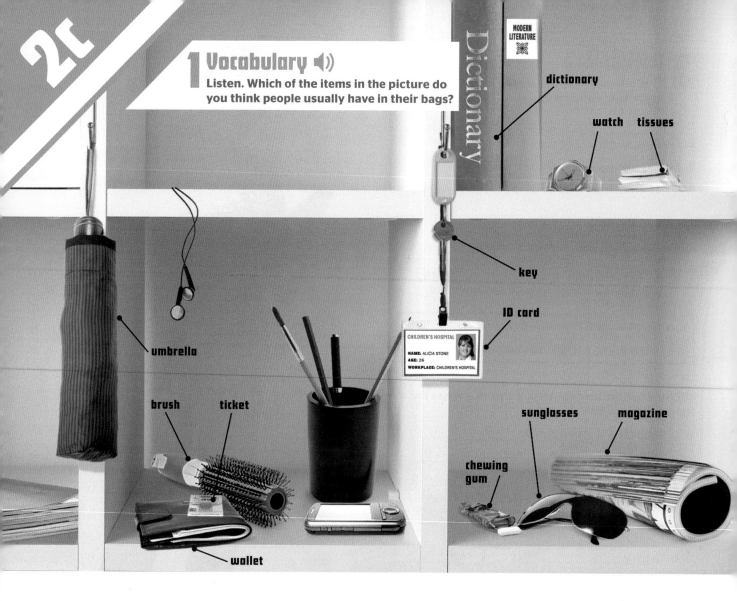

MODERN LITERATURE

Dictionary

dictionary

watch   tissues

key

ID card

umbrella

CHILDREN'S HOSPITAL
NAME: ALICIA STONE
AGE: 26
WORKPLACE: CHILDREN'S HOSPITAL

brush   ticket

sunglasses   magazine

chewing gum

wallet

2 Reading ◀))

Listen, read and answer the questions.

Beth Whose keys are these?

Kate I think they're Mandy's car keys.

Beth Who's Mandy?

Kate She's my sister's friend. She has a Hummer.

Beth What's that?

Kate It's a kind of car.

Beth Is that her car outside?

Kate Yes, it is, her brown Hummer.

1. Is Mandy Beth's friend?
2. Where is Mandy's car?
3. What color is Mandy's car?

Eddie What's that?

Phil It's a watch.

Eddie Yes, it's <u>my</u> watch... in <u>your</u> bag!

Phil Sorry Eddie.

Eddie Where are your watches? You have three or four.

Phil I don't know.

Eddie Well, that watch is expensive and it's my favorite. It's not for school.

Phil You're right, Eddie. Sorry.

1. Whose watch is in the bag?
2. What is expensive?
3. Who is mad?

3 Grammar This/That - These/Those, Plurals → *p. 111*

A. Look at the pictures and read the examples. When do we use *this*, *that*, *these* and *those*?

This is my camera. **These** are my friends.

That is my camera. **Those** are my friends.

B. Look at the table. What do you notice about the formation of plural nouns?

Plural nouns
wallet → wallets
watch → watches
baby → babies

C. Rewrite the sentences in the plural.

1. That's my pencil.

_____

2. This is a bus ticket.

_____

3. That's Kelly's brush.

_____

4. This is an English dictionary.

_____

5. The child has a new magazine.

_____

4 Pronunciation 🔊

A. Listen and repeat. Notice the difference in pronunciation.

a. walle**ts** **b.** key**s** **c.** watch**es**

B. Say these words and check the correct sound. Then listen and check your answers.

	walle**ts** /s/	key**s** /z/	watch**es** /ɪz/
classes			
teachers			
kids			
gadgets			
offices			
laptops			
books			
roommates			
colleges			

A. Listen to the dialogue and choose the correct bag. 🔊

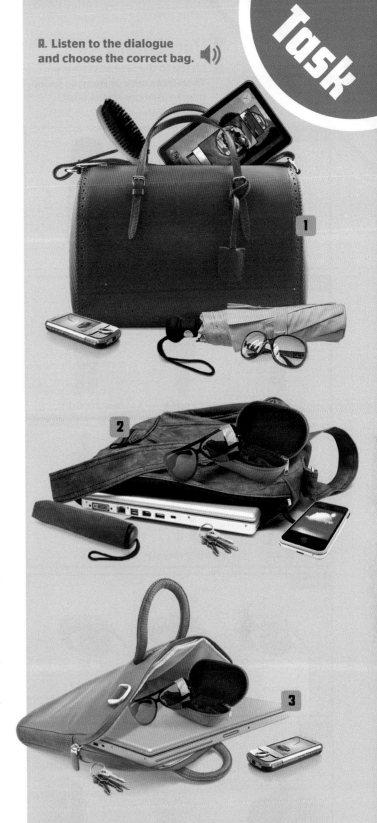

B. Guessing game. Talk in pairs. Go to page 108.

C. Talk in pairs. Discuss what you have in your bag. Answer any questions your partner may have.

❝ *I have my wallet and...*
       What's that? Is it your...? ❞

D. Report to the class what you and your partner have in your bags.

❝ *I have...*
He/She has...
We both have... ❞

1 Vocabulary 🔊

Listen to the words/phrases. Then use some of them to make true sentences about your classmates.

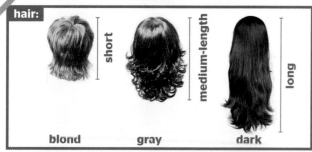

hair:
short | medium-length | long
blond | gray | dark

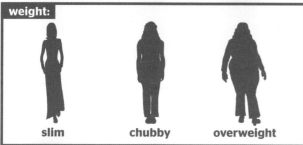

weight:
slim | chubby | overweight

height:
short | medium-height | tall

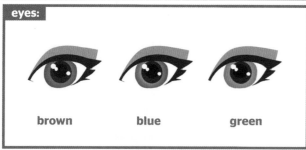

eyes:
brown | blue | green

age:
young/ in his 20s | middle-aged/ in his 50s | old/ in his 80s

general opinion:
handsome / good-looking | beautiful / good-looking

❝ Sally is tall and she has long dark hair. ❞

2 Listening 🔊

A. Look at the pictures and describe the men.

a | b | c

B. Listen to two people talking about a new teacher. Who is Mr. Dupont? Check picture a, b or c.

TIP
Before you listen, always look carefully at the pictures, information, etc. given.

3 Speaking

A. Talk in pairs. Describe the people below.

Harry | Neal | John

Amy | Emma | Sandy

**❝ I think Emma is in her 30s.
No, I think she's in her 40s. ❞**

**B. Guessing game
Talk in pairs.**

Student A: Describe one of the people above to Student B without revealing his/her name.
Student B: Close your book and guess who Student A is talking about from his/her description.
**❝ He's in his fifties and he has short gray hair.
Is it John?**
Yes, it is. ❞

4 Writing A paragraph describing a person

A. Read the e-mail. Which of the topics below does the writer mention about her new roommate?

age

what she looks like

favorite things

name

nationality

job

family

11:00 AM
Home   Gallery   Slideshow

🔍 search

Hi Kelly,

How's it going? Hey, I have a new roommate. Her name is Maria. She's tall and slim and she has long dark hair. She also has beautiful green eyes. She's from Italy and she's an Italian teacher.

B. Read the notes and the paragraph. Add punctuation and capitals.

Punctuation
- Affirmative and negative sentences end with a period (.)
- Questions end with a question mark (?)

Capital letters
Use capital letters:
- at the beginning of a sentence
- with first and last names
- with Mr./Mrs./Miss/Ms./Dr.
- with streets/roads/avenues, etc.
- with cities/countries/nationalities
- with languages
- with the personal pronoun I

husani is twenty years old and he's from egypt he's medium-height and he has dark hair and brown eyes he's a college student and his english is very good husani is my best friend what about your best friend

C. Think of a friend or someone you recently met. What do you know about this person? Complete the table below.

Name: _____

Age: _____

Nationality: _____

Job: _____

Appearance: hair: _____

eyes: _____

height: _____

weight: _____

Family: _____
_____

Other: _____

D. Write a paragraph describing a friend or someone you recently met. Expand on the ideas you noted down in activity C above.

Remember to check punctuation and capital letters in your writing.

25

Vocabulary

A. Cross out the odd word. Then add one more.

1. train – white – pink – brown – _____

2. daughter – sister – grandfather – man – _____

3. tablet – wallet – laptop – camera – _____

4. keys – brush – tissues – hair – _____

5. mad – chubby – short – slim – _____

B. Choose a or b.

1. **A:** What's that?
   B: It's chewing ____.
   a. gum   **b.** card

2. Tonia has ____ brown hair.
   a. handsome   **b.** medium-length

3. **A:** Do you have any brothers or sisters?
   B: No, I'm an only ____.
   a. child   **b.** kid

4. My ____ is in her 30s.
   a. wife   **b.** husband

5. This game is ____. I like it.
   a. terrible   **b.** awesome

Grammar

C. Circle the correct words.

1. What color is your **husband / husband's** car?

2. Where are your **pens / pen's**?

3. Those children **have / has** nice umbrellas.

4. **Who's / Whose** that woman over there?

5. **These / Those** boys over there are my brothers.

6. **Who's / Whose** headphones are these?

7. **This / These** business card is the electrician's.

D. Rewrite the sentences in the plural.

1. This is Tina's brush.

   _____

2. My brother has a purple watch.

   _____

3. That's my dictionary.

   _____

4. That man has a gray smartphone.

   _____

5. Whose magazine is this?

   _____

E. Complete the blanks.

My name's Danny and I **1** _____ a big family. I **2** _____ three daughters and one son. My **3** _____ name **4** _____ Graham and he's five years old. Graham **5** _____ short brown hair but my daughters **6** _____ blond hair. My wife's name is Susan. Her hair **7** _____ blond, too.

Communication

F. Match.

1. What color's your folder?   ☐
2. Where are my sunglasses?   ☐
3. Who is that man outside?   ☐
4. Whose laptop is that?   ☐
5. Is your brother tall?   ☐
6. What's your favorite gadget?   ☐
7. Is that your folder?   ☐

a. My cell.
b. It's yellow and white.
c. No, I have a blue folder.
d. John's.
e. In your backpack.
f. No, he's short.
g. I think he's Kelly's dad.

G. Write questions for the answers given.

1. _____?

   My sister's in her 20s.

2. _____?

   Those are Roger's keys.

3. _____?

   No, he isn't. He's chubby.

4. _____?

   My eyes are green.

5. _____?

   No, I'm not. I'm married.

Self-assessment

Read the following and check the appropriate boxes. For the points you are unsure of, refer back to the relevant sections in the module.

NOW I CAN...

❯ talk and write about members of my family   ☐
❯ identify objects and talk about my possessions   ☐
❯ describe objects   ☐
❯ express my opinion   ☐
❯ describe people's appearance   ☐
❯ write a paragraph describing a person   ☐

MonDaY

TUESDAY

TUE

WEDNESDAY

4

14

Thursday

Sunday

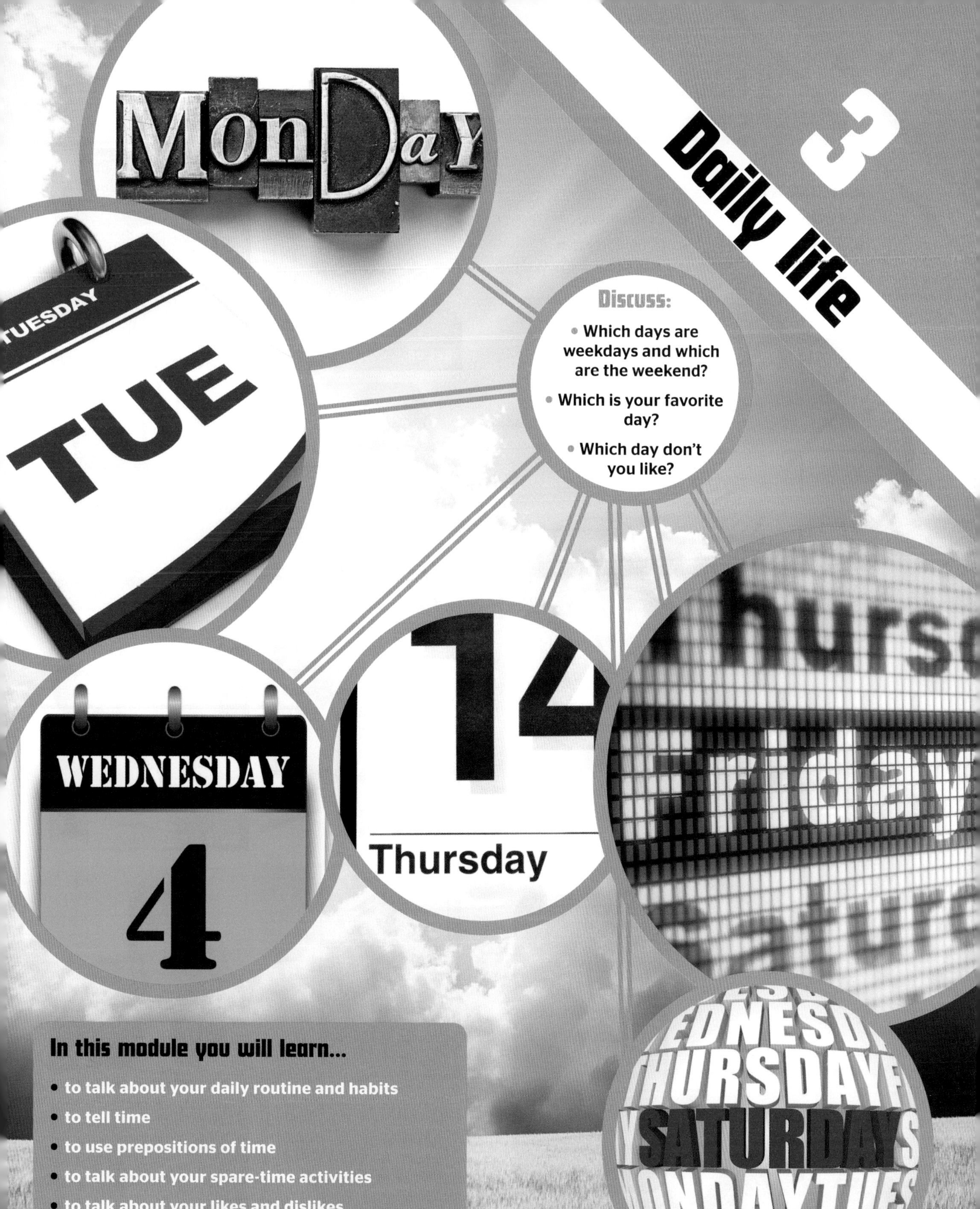

Discuss:
- Which days are weekdays and which are the weekend?
- Which is your favorite day?
- Which day don't you like?

In this module you will learn...

- to talk about your daily routine and habits
- to tell time
- to use prepositions of time
- to talk about your spare-time activities
- to talk about your likes and dislikes
- to express your opinion
- to make suggestions
- to ask and answer different types of questions
- to conduct and report the results of a survey
- about word order
- to write a paragraph about your interests for a social media site

1 Vocabulary & Speaking 🔊

A. Match. Then listen and check your answers.

What time is it?

a. It's ten o'clock.

b. It's ten-oh-five.

c. It's ten fifteen.

d. It's ten thirty.

e. It's ten forty-five.

1 ☐

2 ☐

3 ☐

4 ☐

5 ☐

a.m. = from midnight to noon

p.m. = from noon to midnight

B. Listen to the activities. Then talk in pairs.

get up

take a shower

have breakfast/lunch/dinner

go to work/school

have a class

work from... to...

get home

study

watch TV

go to bed

❝ *I get up at 7:30 every day.*
I get up at 6:30. ❞

2 Reading 🔊

A. Look at the picture and the title of the text. What do you think the text is about? Listen, read and check your answers.

Pastry Patty

Patricia Petit is a college student in Paris but she also works at a pastry store. Every day she gets up early, at 5:15 in the morning. She takes a shower and goes to work. She starts at 6 a.m. and finishes at 9 a.m. She makes lots of different croissants, but her favorite is the chocolate croissant. Patricia doesn't have breakfast at home or at the store. She only has coffee. Then she goes to her classes. She has lunch at her college at about one and then goes to the library to study. After classes, she goes to the pastry store with her friends and they all have croissants!

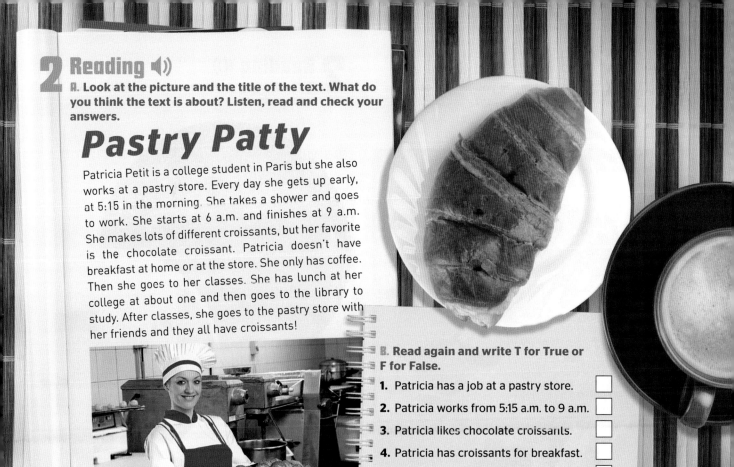

B. Read again and write T for True or F for False.

1. Patricia has a job at a pastry store. ☐
2. Patricia works from 5:15 a.m. to 9 a.m. ☐
3. Patricia likes chocolate croissants. ☐
4. Patricia has croissants for breakfast. ☐
5. Patricia goes home for lunch. ☐
6. Patricia goes home after classes. ☐

3 Grammar Present Simple (affirmative - negative), Prepositions of time → *p. 112*

A. Read the tables. What do you notice about the formation of the third person singular (he, she, it)? How do we form the negative in the Present Simple?

I / You / We / They	
→ work / watch	
→ don't work / don't watch	

He / She / It	
→ works / watches	
→ doesn't work / doesn't watch	

B. Complete with the Present Simple of the verbs in parentheses.

1. My baby sister _____ (not go) to bed at ten o'clock. She _____ (go) to bed at eight thirty.

2. Classes _____ (start) at 9 a.m. and _____ (finish) at about 7 p.m.

3. I _____ (not work) on Saturdays and Sundays.

4. Jack _____ (have) coffee and a croissant for breakfast.

C. Read the table. Make true sentences about your English class using the prepositions of time and the verbs given.

at	7 a.m. / two thirty, etc. noon / night / midnight
on	Monday / Tuesdays, etc. Monday morning, etc. weekdays / the weekend
in	the morning / afternoon / evening

start	finish
(not) have	

66 *I have an English class on Mondays...* **99**

4 Pronunciation 🔊

A. Listen and repeat. Notice the difference in pronunciation.

/s/	start**s**
/z/	lov**es**
/ɪz/	finish**es**

B. Say the words below. In which category would you add them? Listen and check your answers.

lives   likes   works   goes

watches   sends   gets

5 Writing

Think of someone you know well (your mother, father, husband, wife, best friend, etc.) and write a few sentences comparing your daily routines.

I get up at six o'clock. I...

My best friend doesn't get up at six. He gets up at seven o'clock. He...

1 Vocabulary 🔊

Listen. Do you do any of the following?

play

soccer — basketball — tennis — baseball — volleyball — ping-pong

go

bowling — cycling — swimming — running

do

gymnastics — track and field

Learn whole phrases (e.g. verb + noun), not just isolated words.

TIP

2 Reading 🔊

A. Listen and read. Where are the dialogues taking place?

at a park

at a sporting goods store

1 _____

Brad Excuse me. I need a present for a friend. He really likes sports, you see.

Man OK. Does he like all sports?

Brad Umm... Tony plays basketball and...

Man Does he have a ball?

Brad Yes, he does. But it's pretty old. That's a good idea, actually.

Man OK. Basketballs are over here.

2 _____

Jill Hi, Sue. Nice running shoes.

Sue Thanks, they're new.

Jill Do you come here every day?

Sue No, I don't. I go running on Tuesdays, Thursdays and Fridays after work. Let's go running together today. Do you like running?

Jill No, I don't. I hate running. I think it's boring.

Sue I think it's fun.

B. Read again and complete the sentences.

1. _____ likes basketball.

2. Brad's present for Tony is a _____.

3. Sue has new _____.

4. Sue goes to the park _____ days a week.

5. _____ doesn't like running at all. She thinks it's _____.

3 Grammar Present Simple (Yes/No questions and short answers) → p. 112

A. Read the examples. How do we form short answers in the Present Simple?

> • **Do** you **go** swimming every day?
> Yes, I/we **do**. / No, I/we **don't**.
>
> • **Does** he/she **do** gymnastics?
> Yes, he/she **does**. / No, he/she **doesn't**.

B. Complete the dialogues with the Present Simple of the verbs in parentheses. Give short answers where possible.

A: 1 _____ you and your friends _____ (play) baseball every day?

B: No, **2** _____. We **3** _____ (play) on Wednesdays after school.

A: What about on weekends?

B: We **4** _____ (not play) baseball on weekends. We **5** _____ (go) bowling. Let's go bowling together. **6** _____ you _____ (like) bowling?

A: No, **7** _____. I **8** _____ (like) ping-pong.

B: My brother **9** _____ (play) ping-pong.

A: Really? **10** _____ your brother _____ (play) on the weekend?

B: Yes, **11** _____.

A: That's great. Where's your brother now?

4 Listening 🔊

Listen to three short dialogues and choose a or b.

1. The boy ____.
  a. plays soccer
  b. watches soccer on TV

2. The woman goes cycling ____.
  a. on weekdays
  b. on the weekend

3. The boys think ____ is boring.
  a. tennis
  b. tennis on TV

5 Speaking

A. Do you like these sports? How much? Write the emoticon under each one.

| :-) Yes, very much! | :-I It's OK. | :-(No! |

B. Talk in pairs or small groups. Ask each other about different sports and then make a suggestion to do something together.

Do you like...?	*I like... very much.*
Yes, I do.	*I really like...*
It's OK.	*I love...*
No, I don't.	*I think it's fun.*
Let's... after school/work.	*I don't like... very much.*
That's a good idea.	*I don't like... at all.*
No, sorry.	*I hate...*
	I think it's boring.

> We use **Let's + base form of the verb** to suggest something.
>
> *Let's play volleyball together.*

31

1 Vocabulary & Speaking 🔊

Listen. Then talk in pairs. Do you do any of these activities in your spare time? When do you do them? What else do you do?

go to the movies

read the newspaper

go to the gym

hang out with friends

listen to music

play video games

go shopping

go to a game

go for coffee

❝ I go to the gym every day after work.

I go to the gym, too. I go on Wednesdays and on the weekend. ❞

2 Reading 🔊

A. Read the text quickly and match the questions a-c with the paragraphs 1-3. Then listen and check your answers.

a. Do they work alone?

b. Do they work long hours?

c. What do game testers do?

LIFE AS A... GAME TESTER!

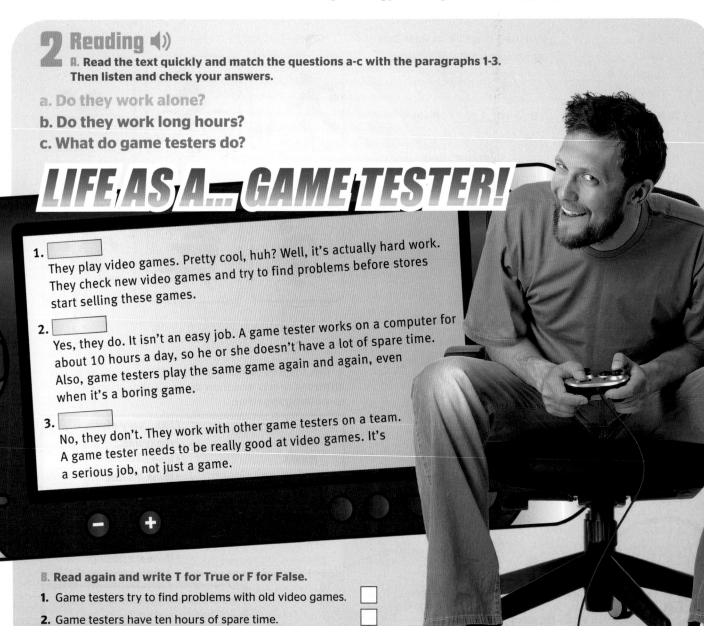

1. [ ] They play video games. Pretty cool, huh? Well, it's actually hard work. They check new video games and try to find problems before stores start selling these games.

2. [ ] Yes, they do. It isn't an easy job. A game tester works on a computer for about 10 hours a day, so he or she doesn't have a lot of spare time. Also, game testers play the same game again and again, even when it's a boring game.

3. [ ] No, they don't. They work with other game testers on a team. A game tester needs to be really good at video games. It's a serious job, not just a game.

B. Read again and write T for True or F for False.

1. Game testers try to find problems with old video games. [ ]

2. Game testers have ten hours of spare time. [ ]

3. Game testers don't play boring video games. [ ]

4. The job of a game tester is hard. [ ]

3 Grammar Present Simple (Wh-questions)
→ p. 112

A. Read the examples. What's the difference between Yes/No questions and Wh-questions? What's the difference between When and What time?

> A: **Do** you go to the movies?
> B: Yes, I do.
>
> A: **When** do you go?
> B: On the weekend.
>
> A: **What time** do you go?
> B: At eight o'clock in the evening.

B. Circle the correct words.

1. A: **When / What** do you do on weekends?

   B: I hang out with my friends.

2. A: What time **Greg gets / does Greg get** home?

   B: At six o'clock.

3. A: **How / Where** do you go after work?

   B: I go home.

4. A: **When / What time** does your sister play ping-pong?

   B: In the evenings.

5. A: What sports **you play / do you play**?

   B: Soccer and baseball.

4 Intonation 🔊

A. Listen and repeat. What's the difference between questions a and b?

a. Do you go shopping?

b. When do you go shopping?

B. Listen and repeat. Is the intonation rising ↗ or falling ↘?

1. Does Sally listen to music?

2. What time do you go to the gym?

3. Is this video game boring?

4. Do you go for coffee every day?

5. Where does your brother live?

6. What magazines do you like?

A. Listen to someone answering questions for a survey and complete the survey below. 🔊

TIP
Before you listen, read the questions and answer choices carefully and make sure you don't have any unknown words.

SURVEY: SPARE TIME

Gender: Male ☐ Female ☐   **Age:** _26_

Do you have a lot of spare time?

Yes ☐   No ☐

What do you do in your spare time?

play sports ☐
hang out with friends ☐
go shopping ☐
go to the movies ☐
play video games ☐
watch DVDs ☐
read magazines ☐
other _____

What's your favorite spare-time activity?

_____
_____

When do you do it?

Mon ☐   Tues ☐   Wed ☐   Thurs ☐   Fri ☐
Sat ☐   Sun ☐

Do you do this activity alone or with others?

alone ☐   with others ☐

Who do you do it with?

family ☐   friends ☐   colleagues ☐

B. Work in pairs. Ask your partner the questions in the survey above and keep notes of his/her answers.

C. Report your partner's answers to the class.
❝ ... has /doesn't have a lot of spare time.
In his/her spare time, he/she...
He/She also... but he/she doesn't...
His/Her favorite activity is reading/playing/going...
He/She... ❞

33

1 Vocabulary 🔊

Listen to the TV shows, read the TV guide and answer the questions.

sports

sitcom

documentary

the news

soap opera

game show

MORRELL   NORTH   RANDALL   ALDER

WASHINGTON COLLEGE

the weather

talk show

talent show

NBC

CBS

+25°C 23 APR 2011 SAT

7:30 **LIVE** Soccer
D.C. United vs. L.A. Galaxy

8:15 Let's make a deal

9:15 MOVIE Iron Man

11:00 American Idol

9:00 Wild Kingdom

10:00 Days of Our Lives

11:00 News and Weather

11:30 The Tonight Show
with Jay Leno

- Can you find any of the TV shows in the TV guide?
- On what channel?
- What time are they on?

2 Listening 🔊

Listen and answer the questions. Choose a or b.

1. What's on TV?

   a. a talk show

   b. a game show

2. What does the man like?

   a. sports

   b. documentaries

3. What does Kim watch every day?

   a. a soap opera

   b. the news

3 Speaking

**Talk in groups of three about TV shows.
Use the ideas below.**

- What kind of TV shows / you / like?
- What / be / favorite show?
- What channel / be / on?
- What time / be / on?
- What day / be / on?
- Where / you / watch / it?
- Who / you / watch it with?

66 *What kind of TV shows do you like?*
   I like talent shows.
   Me too. I think they're fun.
What's your favorite...?
   ...
   ...
What time is it on?
   It's on at... 99

4 Writing A profile for a social media site

A. Read the profile below and look at the pictures 1-5. Which of these activities does Janice do in her spare time?

meetyourfriends.com

Home   Profile   Account ▾

Janice Wilson
jwilson445@gmail.com

Interests
I have lots of friends and we hang out a lot. We go to the movies, we go for coffee and we go bowling together, too. I also like shopping. I go every Saturday with my friends. When I stay home, I watch a lot of TV. My favorite shows are talk shows and talent shows, but I don't watch documentaries. I watch a lot of sports, too. I love tennis and I watch the U.S. Open every year. I don't play tennis, but I exercise at home. I run on the treadmill every day.

Info

Friends

B. Read the note and make sentences by putting the words in the correct order.

> **Word order**
> In English, we always put the subject of a sentence before the verb.
>
> **Subject + verb**
>
> I   go   swimming with my friends.
> Brad   doesn't study   on the weekend.

1. don't / I / operas / watch / soap

_____

2. we / together / ping-pong / play

_____

3. friends / evening / running / every / my / go

_____

4. home / at / go / midnight / I

_____

C. Think of what your interests are, what you do in your spare time, when and who with. Write some notes in the table below.

activities you do outside the home:	_____
activities you do at home:	_____

D. Write a paragraph describing your interests for a social media website. Use your notes from activity C above.

> **TIP**
> Before you start writing, think of the ideas you are going to write about and keep some notes. This will help you organize your writing.

Vocabulary

A. Match.

1. go   **a.** a soap opera
2. read   **b.** a shower
3. go to   **c.** shopping
4. do   **d.** track and field
5. watch   **e.** the newspaper
6. take   **f.** bed

B. Complete with the words in the box.

guide   hangs   cycling   from   treadmill   study

1. Ms. White works _____ 9:30 a.m. to 5:30 p.m.

2. After school, I go home and _____.

3. My brother _____ out with his friends every weekend.

4. Where's the TV _____?

5. **A:** I have a _____ at home and I exercise every evening.

   B: Really? I go _____ with my friends in the evenings.

Grammar

C. Complete with the Present Simple of the verbs in parentheses.

1. Kelly _____ (not get up) at nine. She _____ (get up) at eight.

2. I think Paul _____ (need) a new car.

3. My husband _____ (start) work at seven and _____ (finish) at three.

4. Mary and Linda _____ (not stay) home on Sundays. They _____ (go) swimming.

5. I _____ (not watch) talent shows. I think they're boring.

D. Complete with *in*, *on* or *at*.

1. Jerry plays baseball _____ Tuesdays and Thursdays.

2. Tina goes for coffee _____ Sunday mornings.

3. We don't go running _____ night.

4. Do you go to the movies _____ the weekend?

5. I get home _____ about four o'clock _____ the afternoon.

Communication

E. Complete the questions for the answers below.

1. **A:** _____?

   B: It's twelve thirty.

2. **A:** _____ lunch?

   B: At one o'clock.

3. **A:** _____ to the gym?

   B: On Mondays and Fridays.

4. **A:** _____ soccer?

   B: No, he doesn't. He plays tennis.

5. **A:** _____ in the evenings?

   B: I listen to music.

F. Complete the dialogues. Choose a or b.

1. **A:** I like volleyball very much.

   B: ____
   a. Actually, I really hate it, too.
   b. Me too.

2. **A:** ____

   B: That's a good idea.
   a. Let's go to a basketball game.
   b. I think basketball is fun.

3. **A:** ____

   B: Yes, he loves bowling.
   a. Does Danny go bowling?
   b. When does Danny go bowling?

4. **A:** What's on?

   B: ____
   a. At ten.
   b. A game show.

Self-assessment

Read the following and check the appropriate boxes. For the points you are unsure of, refer back to the relevant sections in the module.

NOW I CAN...

- talk about my daily routine and habits ☐
- tell time ☐
- use prepositions of time ☐
- talk about my spare-time activities ☐
- talk about my likes and dislikes ☐
- express my opinion ☐
- make suggestions ☐
- ask and answer different types of questions ☐
- write a paragraph about my interests for a social media site ☐

bedroom

Discuss:

- Where are the following in your house?

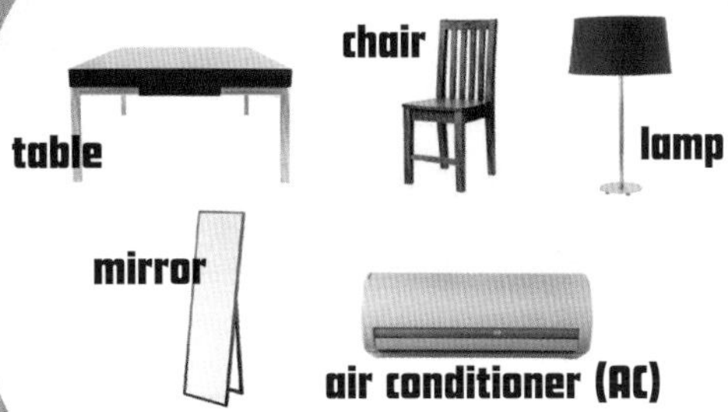

table

chair

lamp

mirror

air conditioner (AC)

- Do you like your home?
- Is there anything you want to change?

living room

bathroom

In this module you will learn...

- to talk about daily routines and habits
- to talk about frequency
- to refer to the location of objects
- to speculate about possibilities
- to describe a room
- to talk about furniture, appliances and parts of a house
- to read and understand house advertisements and plans
- to collaborate with someone to reach a decision
- to describe your house/apartment
- to write a description of your house/apartment

kitchen

1 Vocabulary 🔊
Listen. Do you do housework?

do/wash the dishes

take out the trash

vacuum

wash the car

do the laundry

cook

mow the lawn

go grocery shopping

2 Reading 🔊
A. Listen and read. Where would you find a text like this? Who is it for?

My guide to simple housework
by NATALIE POWERS

Who likes housework? Not me, but I like my house to be nice and clean. So, here are some tips:

Floors
I usually vacuum every Friday and it's really easy. It takes about 15 minutes because I don't have a lot of furniture. I also want to buy a Vacuuming Robot. My sister has one. She turns it on in the morning before work and her floors are always clean.

Kitchen
I can't stand a dirty and messy kitchen. So, I never leave dirty pots and pans for later. I clean as I cook, and I always tell my family to fill the dishwasher when they finish lunch. It helps.

Yard
We have a big yard but I don't have time for it. I don't often mow the lawn, it's a job my kids usually do. And they like it. One of our neighbors has a Robot Mower. It's pretty cool, so check it out!

B. Read again and answer the questions.

1. When does Natalie vacuum?
2. Does Natalie have a lot of furniture in her house?
3. Who has a Vacuuming Robot?
4. What does Natalie hate?
5. What does her family do when they finish lunch?
6. Who mows the lawn?
7. Who has a Robot Mower?

3 Grammar Adverbs of frequency → *p. 113*

A. Look at the pie charts and read the examples. What do you notice about the position of adverbs of frequency?

Roger **never** cooks.
Emily doesn't **often** wash the car.
Paul is **always** late for dinner.

B. Put the words in order to make sentences.

1. never / Greg / listens / music / to

_____

2. does / Helen / always / dishes / dinner / after / the

_____

3. sister / often / My / watch / doesn't / soap operas

_____

4. mom / on / usually / My / vacuums / Saturday mornings

_____

C. Say two things you always do and two things you never do on Saturdays.

66 *I always clean the house on Saturday mornings. I never stay home on Saturday evenings.* 99

4 Listening 🔊

A. Listen to Fiona answering questions for a survey. Who is Mark?

a. Fiona's brother   **b.** Fiona's husband

B. Listen again and check what Fiona and Mark do.

	Fiona	Mark
do the dishes	☐	☐
vacuum	☐	☐
wash the car	☐	☐
do the laundry	☐	☐
go grocery shopping	☐	☐

5 Speaking

Talk in pairs. Discuss who does the housework in your house.

66 *In my house, I usually...*
I never... but I often...
My... sometimes... 99

1 Vocabulary

A. Listen. What other items of furniture do you have in your house?

B. Listen. Then look at the pictures on the left and make sentences using the prompts.

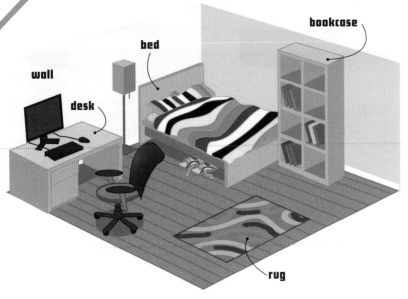

wall
bed
bookcase
desk
rug

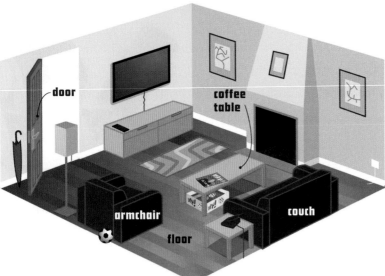

door
coffee table
armchair
couch
floor

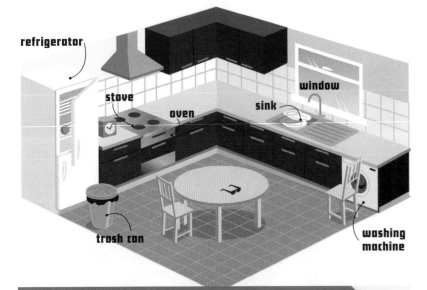

refrigerator
stove
oven
sink
window
trash can
washing machine

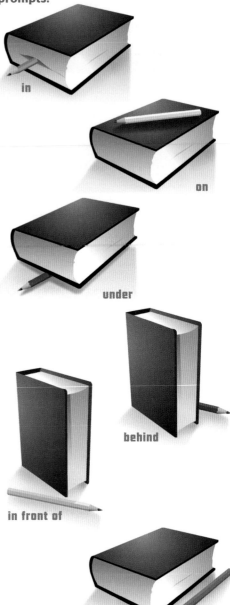

in

on

under

behind

in front of

next to

computer – desk
running shoes – bed
umbrella – door
green lamp – armchair
TV – wall
ball – armchair
clock – refrigerator
chair – washing machine
dishes – sink

TIP

Learn new vocabulary by putting words in groups (e.g. furniture found in particular rooms or furniture and appliances). This way, it is easier to remember them.

66 *The computer is on the desk.* 99

2 Reading 🔊

A. Listen and read. Does Mike find all his things?

John Oops!

Mike Watch out!

John Sorry!

Mike Oh no! Look at my things. They're all over the floor! And my coffee, too!

John Let me help you.

Mike Where's my cell phone?

John It's under the kitchen table, and here's your notebook. Sorry, Mike.

Mike Now, where's my black pen?

John Maybe it's behind the door.

Mike It's not. Oh, where is it? I need it.

John Perhaps it's in the trash can.

Mike Yes, here it is. That's funny!

John Now, sit down. Do you want some fresh coffee?

Mike Sure. Thanks, John.

John Don't mention it!

B. Read again and correct the sentences.

1. Mike and John are in the living room.
2. Mike's coffee is on the table.
3. Mike's cell is in the trash can.
4. Mike's pen is behind the door.

3 Intonation 🔊

Listen and repeat. Notice the intonation and rhythm.

1. **A:** Where's my notebook?
   B: It's on the coffee table.

2. **A:** Where's the black umbrella?
   B: It's behind the armchair.

3. **A:** Where are my running shoes?
   B: They're in the bathroom.

4. **A:** Where's the new lamp?
   B: It's next to the TV.

4 Speaking

Talk in groups of three. The items in the box are missing from the picture. Discuss and guess where they are. Then go to page 110 and check your answers.

| cell phone | sunglasses | newspaper | tablet | backpack |

66 *Where's the...?*
   Maybe/Perhaps it's... Where are the...?
   I think they're... 99

5 Speaking & Writing

A. Talk in pairs. Ask each other about the furniture and things you have in your bedroom.

66 *Do you have a clock in your bedroom?*
   Yes, I do.
Where is it?
   It's next to my bed. 99

B. Write a few sentences about the furniture and things you have in your bedroom.

In my bedroom, I have...

1 Vocabulary 🔊

Listen. Do you live in a house or an apartment?

apartment · upstairs · house · downstairs

balcony · garage

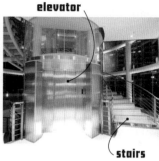

elevator · stairs

2 Reading 🔊

A. Look at the advertisements and the picture. Guess who the people are and what they are talking about. Then listen, read and check your answers.

B. Read the advertisements and the dialogue again. Which house do they decide to see?

DONOVAN ROAD, KENSINGTON

FOR RENT

2-story house, 1,000ft²
furnished
$665 per month

2 bedrooms with large closets
2 bathrooms
modern kitchen
front and backyard

COOPER STREET, KENSINGTON

FOR RENT

2-story house, 1,500ft²
furnished
$780 per month

3 bedrooms, 1 bathroom
large kitchen
backyard
garage

Mandy	Hi, I'm Mandy. How can I help you?
Woman	Hello. I need a house to rent, for me and my roommate.
Mandy	How many bedrooms?
Woman	Two. But we don't mind an extra bedroom.
Mandy	OK. There's a house on Donovan Road and a house on Cooper Street. The Donovan house has a front and backyard.
Woman	That sounds nice. Does it have a large kitchen?
Mandy	Well, not really. But there are two bathrooms - a large bathroom upstairs and a small bathroom downstairs.
Woman	Is there a garage?
Mandy	No, there isn't.
Woman	Oh, that's a problem. My roommate has a car, you see.
Mandy	OK, let's go and see the other house, then.
Woman	What, now?
Mandy	Yes, why not?

C. Read again and write T for True or F for False.

1. The woman doesn't want a 3-bedroom house. ☐

2. The house on Cooper Street doesn't have a front yard. ☐

3. There is a large kitchen in the house on Donovan Road. ☐

4. There is a large bathroom downstairs in the house on Donovan Road. ☐

5. The woman's roommate needs a house with a garage. ☐

3 Grammar There is / There are, Articles

→ *p. 113*

A. Read the examples and make sentences with there is/are.

> **There's** a balcony upstairs.
> **There isn't** a balcony downstairs.
>
> **Is there** a garage? → **Yes, there is.**
>   → **No, there isn't.**
>
> **There aren't** three bedrooms upstairs.
> **There are** only two.
>
> **Are there** big windows in the kitchen? → **Yes, there are.**
>   → **No, there aren't.**

B. Read the examples. What's the difference between *a(n)* and *the*?

> In our living room, there's **a** couch and **an** armchair.
>
> **The** couch is new but **the** armchair is old.

C. Complete with *a(n)* or *the*.

1. There is _____ table on our balcony. _____ table is next to _____ door.

2. **A:** There's _____ cell phone on _____ couch.

   B: Is _____ cell phone white?

   A: Yes, it is.

   B: Maybe it's Julie's. She has _____ white cell phone.

3. There are two lamps in _____ living room, _____ small lamp and _____ big lamp. _____ big lamp is on _____ floor.

4. **A:** Excuse me. Where is _____ elevator?

   B: There is _____ elevator next to _____ stairs.

   A: OK, thank you.

A. Listen to two college students deciding which apartment to rent and choose plan 1 or 2. 🔊

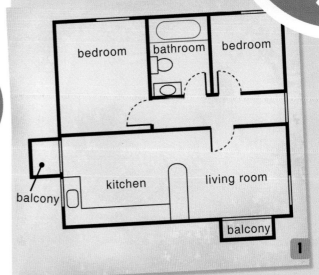

B. Talk in pairs. Imagine that you and your partner are going to be roommates. Look at the plans above. Discuss and decide which apartment you are going to rent.

> 66 *So, what do you think?*
>   ***Well, there's a... in apartment 1, but in apartment 2...***
> *You're right. Apartment 1 also has...*
>   ***The... is small. Is that a problem?***
> *I don't know, I like...*
>   ***OK, let's rent apartment...*** 99

C. Report your decision to the class and give reasons.

> 66 *We want to rent apartment... because...* 99

43

1 Vocabulary & Speaking 🔊

A. Listen. What are the next five ordinals?

1st	first	11th	eleventh
2nd	second	12th	twelfth
3rd	third	13th	thirteenth
4th	fourth	14th	fourteenth
5th	fifth	15th	fifteenth
6th	sixth	16th	sixteenth
7th	seventh	17th	seventeenth
8th	eighth	18th	eighteenth
9th	ninth	19th	nineteenth
10th	tenth	20th	twentieth
		21st	twenty-first

B. Talk in pairs. Hold a conversation using ideas from the dialogue below.

> 66 *Where do you live?*
> *I live in Mayfair.*
> *Where exactly? What's your address?*
> *133 Bell Road.*
> *Really? I live on Bell Road, too. At number 157.*
> *Do you live in a house or in an apartment?*
> *I live in an apartment.*
> *What floor do you live on?*
> *On the 24th floor.* 99

I live **at** 133 Bell Road.

I live **in** an apartment / Mayfair / London / Canada.

I live **on** Bell Road / the 24th floor.

---

2 Listening 🔊

Listen and choose the correct picture.

1. Where does Elisa live?

2. What is Gary's address?

3 Writing A description of a house / an apartment

A. Marcia wants to rent her apartment for the summer. Below is a paragraph she has written for a website. Read the description and complete the information form.

Vacation Rentals

Search for [   ] 🔍

My apartment is at 456 Columbus Avenue, on the 5th floor. It's 650ft². It's small but cozy. There are two bedrooms, a kitchen, a small living room and a bathroom. There's also a large balcony with a great view of the city.

In my living room, there are two armchairs, a couch and a big TV screen on the wall. It's fantastic! The kitchen has a new refrigerator, a microwave, a table and four chairs. The large bedroom has a double bed and the small bedroom has a single bed.

Address [   ]

House or Apartment? [   ]

Floor? [   ]

Big or small? [   ]

Number of bedrooms? [   ]

Number of bathrooms? [   ]

Balcony?   **yes** [ ]   **no** [ ]

Yard?   **yes** [ ]   **no** [ ]

Furnished?   **yes** [ ]   **no** [ ]

AC?   **yes** [ ]   **no** [ ]

TV?   **yes** [ ]   **no** [ ]

B. Read the note and use the prompts to make sentences.

When writing a description of a house / an apartment, don't forget to use:

- **there is / there are** and **have / has.**
  There are two bathrooms in my house.
  My house has two bathrooms.
- **commas** and **and** to list things.
  In the kitchen there's a refrigerator, an oven and a microwave.

1. my bedroom: bed / desk / TV

In my bedroom _____

_____

My bedroom _____

_____

2. my house: three bedrooms / living room / bathroom / modern kitchen

In my house _____

My house _____

C. Imagine you want to rent your house/apartment for the summer. Copy and complete the information form in activity A and talk in pairs. Discuss the questions given.

- *Where do you live?*
- *Do you live in a house or in an apartment?*
- *What floor do you live on?*
- *Is your house/apartment big or small?*
- *How many bedrooms/bathrooms are there?*
- *Is there a balcony/yard?*
- *Is your house/apartment furnished?*
- *Do you have an air conditioner / a TV?*

D. Write a description of your house/apartment for the Vacation Rentals website. Use the ideas you discussed in activity C.

When you finish writing, edit your work. Check:
- capital letters
- punctuation
- spelling
- vocabulary
- prepositions
- grammar
- word order

TIP

Vocabulary

A. Write:

1. three things you would find in a living room.

   _____, _____, _____

2. three things you would find in a kitchen.

   _____, _____, _____

3. three things you would find in a bedroom.

   _____, _____, _____

B. Complete the phrases.

1. _____ the laundry

2. _____ the trash

3. _____ grocery shopping

4. _____ the lawn

5. _____ the dishes

6. _____ housework

C. Circle the correct words.

1. There's a big clock **behind / on** the wall.

2. Is the English dictionary **next to / in** the TV?

3. There's a small rug **in front / behind** of the washing machine.

4. The croissants are **in / on** the coffee table.

5. I think your running shoes are **next / under** your bed.

Grammar

D. Rewrite the sentences using the adverbs of frequency in parentheses.

1. Mrs. Dale does the laundry on Saturdays. (sometimes)

   _____

2. I don't cook on the weekend. (often)

   _____

3. When do you clean the house? (usually)

   _____

4. My brother studies in the evenings. (never)

   _____

5. I'm late for my English class. (always)

   _____

E. Complete.

I live in **1** _____ beautiful house in Fairview. It's pretty big and it **2** _____ two floors. My bedroom is upstairs. **3** _____'s a bed, a desk and a TV in my room. I also have **4** _____ old couch next to the window. I always sit on **5** _____ couch and watch TV in the evenings. Next to **6** _____ bedroom there's **7** _____ small bathroom. There **8** _____ two bathrooms in the house but **9** _____ big bathroom is downstairs. Downstairs **10** _____'s also a living room and a kitchen. **11** _____ kitchen is very modern.

Communication

F. Complete the questions for the answers below.

1. **A:** _____?

   B: At 52 Maple Street.

2. **A:** _____?

   B: No, never.

3. **A:** _____?

   B: Perhaps the newspaper is on the coffee table.

4. **A:** _____?

   B: On the 7th floor.

5. **A:** _____?

   B: Yes, there is, a front and backyard.

6. **A:** _____?

   B: There are three bedrooms in my house.

7. **A:** _____?

   B: No, there's only one bathroom and it's downstairs.

Self-assessment

Read the following and check the appropriate boxes. For the points you are unsure of, refer back to the relevant sections in the module.

now i can...

❯ talk about daily routines and habits	☐
❯ talk about frequency	☐
❯ refer to the location of objects	☐
❯ speculate about possibilities	☐
❯ describe a room	☐
❯ talk about furniture, appliances and parts of a house	☐
❯ describe my house/apartment	☐
❯ write a description of my house/apartment	☐

Discuss:

- Can you match the pictures with the names of the cities?
  Rio de Janeiro   Los Angeles
  Cairo   Moscow   Sydney
  Beijing

- Are any of them capital cities?

- Which is the biggest?

- Which is your favorite city?

In this module you will learn...

- to talk about the modes of transportation you use
- to talk about your abilities
- to refer to the location of places in a town/city
- to read a map
- to ask for, give and follow directions
- some useful vocabulary related to the environment
- to collaborate with others, discuss ideas and reach a decision
- to express your opinion
- to talk about places in your town/city
- how to avoid repetition when writing
- to write a description of your town/city

47

1 Vocabulary 🔊

Listen. How else can you get around in your town/city?

drive a car

ride a bike

ride a motorcycle

walk

take a cab/taxi

take the subway

take the bus

2 Reading 🔊

A. How do you think a businesswoman, a teacher and a college student get around the city? Listen, read and check your answers.

HOW DO YOU GET AROUND THE CITY?

People don't always use the same mode of transportation. They think of the traffic, the time they have, the money, the weather, etc. Write and tell us how you get around.

POSTED BY:
NANCY
13:46

I'm a businesswoman and I work downtown. I live outside the city and take the train every morning. From the station, I usually take a bus to my office or a cab when I'm late. My mornings aren't easy, but I can't drive so I don't have a car.

POSTED BY:
DEREK
18:58

I'm an elementary school teacher. I live near the school, so I can walk to work. When I want to go shopping or go out with friends, I ride my bike. There are lots of bicycle lanes around the city. I don't use public transportation very often, only when there's bad weather.

POSTED BY:
MARK
21:05

I'm a student, but my apartment is far from my college. I sometimes take the bus to get there. When there's a lot of traffic, I take the subway. Sometimes, friends give me a ride home in the evenings. I can't buy a car right now, but I really want to get a motorcycle.

B. Read again and write N for Nancy, D for Derek or M for Mark.

1. This person doesn't live in the city. ☐
2. This person doesn't need a lot of time to get to his/her school/work. ☐
3. This person sometimes gets a ride from others. ☐
4. This person sometimes takes a taxi. ☐
5. This person wants to change the way he/she gets around the city. ☐
6. This person doesn't often use public transportation. ☐
7. This person uses two modes of transportation in the morning. ☐

3 Speaking

Discuss the following:

• How do you get to work/school/the gym, etc.?
• Do you often use public transportation?
• Is it easy to get around your neighborhood/town/city on a bike?
• How do you get around when the weather is bad?
• Is there a lot of traffic in your town/city?
• Do you have a car? Do you use it a lot?

4 Grammar The verb *can* → *p. 113*

A. Read the examples. When do we use *can* and when do we use *can't*?

I He/She/It We/You/They	**can**	run fast.
I He/She/It We/You/They	**can't**	run fast.
Can	I he/she/it we/you/they	run fast?
Yes,	I he/she/it we/you/they	**can.**
No,	I he/she/it we/you/they	**can't.**

B. Complete with *can* and the words in parentheses. Give short answers where possible.

1. Carol starts work at 7 a.m. but she's usually late.
She _____ (not get) up early in the mornings.

2. A: _____ (you / speak) French?
B: No, _____, but I _____ (speak) Spanish.

3. A: _____ (your sister / drive)?
B: No, _____. She's only fourteen!

4. A: Peter loves sports. He _____ (play) soccer and basketball well.
B: Really? _____ (he / play) baseball well, too?
A: Baseball? Oh, I don't know about that.

5. A: _____ (the children / swim)?
B: Yes, _____.
A: Great! Let's go swimming together.

C. Group survey

Work in groups of four. Look at the table below and complete the left column with your own ideas.
Then ask each other questions and note down the answers. Finally, report your group's answers to the class.

Can you...?	YOU	Student 1:	Student 2:	Student 3:
drive a car				
ride a bike				
ride a motorcycle				

5 Listening ◀))

A. Listen to somebody talking on the radio. What is he talking about? Choose a, b or c.

a. a bicycle race downtown
b. what people can do downtown today
c. the traffic downtown

B. Listen again and write T for True or F for False.

1. There are lots of people in the stores today. ☐
2. Drivers can't use Main Street. ☐
3. There is a lot of traffic on Park Avenue. ☐
4. It's a good idea to walk around the city today. ☐

1 Vocabulary 🔊

Listen. Then find these places on the map below.

bank

police station

gas station

supermarket

shopping mall

airport

movie theater

hotel

parking lot

coffee shop

2 Reading 🔊

A. Listen, read and name the two shopping malls on the map below.

Woman: Excuse me, is this North City Mall?

Man: No, this is Shoppers World. North City Mall is on Bywater Street.

Woman: Thank you. Now, I need to find a cab.

Man: Don't take a cab. Walk there.

Woman: Well, I don't know my way around.

Man: Don't worry. It's only a ten-minute walk.

Woman: Oh, OK. How can I get there?

Man: Go down this road and turn left at the traffic lights. That's Bywater Street. Go straight and the mall is on your right, across from the police station.

Woman: OK, thanks.

Man: No problem.

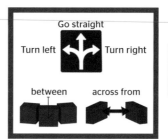

Go straight

Turn left   Turn right

between   across from

a ten-minute walk

~~a ten-minutes walk~~

B. Read again and write T for True or F for False.

1. The woman wants to go to Shoppers World. ☐
2. The woman takes a cab to the mall. ☐
3. It takes ten minutes to walk to the mall. ☐
4. The police station is next to the mall. ☐
5. The police station is on Bywater Street. ☐

Bywater Street

Park Road

Green Street

Fremont Avenue

P

3 Grammar Imperative → p. 113

Read the examples and complete the sentences 1-5 with the correct form of the verbs in the box.

← Go straight.
Don't stop.

Don't turn right. →
Stop and wait!

not drive	do	not use	go	turn
not watch	take			

1. **A:** How do I get to the gas station?

   B: _____ down this street and _____ right at the coffee shop. The gas station is on your left, between the supermarket and the bank.

2. _____ your car to work. _____ the bus.

3. _____ TV now. It's late!

4. Maria! Please _____ the dishes. I don't have time.

5. **A:** _____ the elevator. It doesn't work.

   B: Oh, OK.

4 Listening 🔊))

Look at the map below and listen to three short dialogues. Where do the people want to go?

1. _____ 2. _____ 3. _____

5 Speaking

Talk in pairs. Look at the map below.

Student A: Imagine that you are at the traffic lights on Gold Street. You want to go to Joe's Coffee Shop, but you don't know where it is. Ask Student B for directions. Use the phrases in the box.

> How can/do I get to...?
> Excuse me, where's...?
> Excuse me, is... near here?
> Is it far?

Student B: Choose one of the orange squares on the map to be Joe's Coffee Shop. Don't show Student A which square you have chosen. Imagine you are at the traffic lights on Gold Street. Give Student A directions. Use the phrases in the box.

> Go down...
> Go straight.
> Turn left/right at the hotel / traffic lights, etc.
> It's on your left/right.
> It's next to / between / across from...

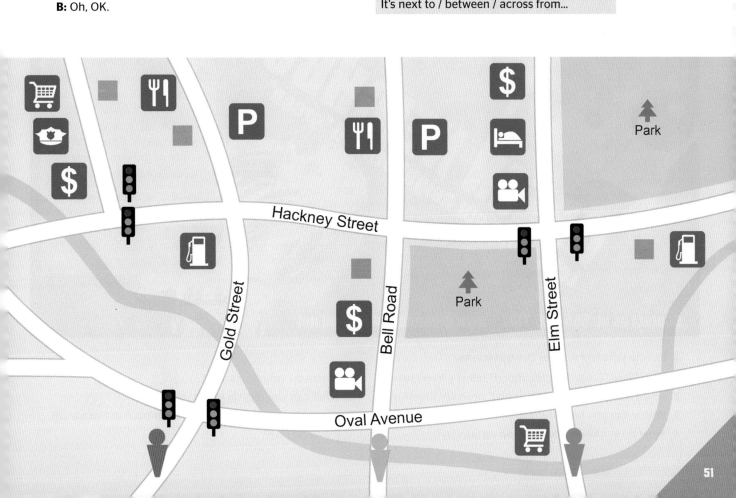

Hackney Street

Gold Street

Bell Road

Park

Elm Street

Park

Oval Avenue

1 Vocabulary ◀))
Listen. Do you do any of these activities?

HELP PROTECT THE ENVIRONMENT!

Plant trees.

Throw trash in trash cans.

Use recycling bins. Recycle newspapers, magazines, bottles and cans.

Save energy. Turn off lights.

Save water. Turn off the faucet.

Use public transportation.

2 Reading ◀))

A. Look at the poster about the organization "Green Neighborhood" and read the titles. What do you think happens at these events? Listen, read and check your answers.

GREEN NEIGHBORHOOD
Let's make our neighborhood "green"

Garage Sale
Don't throw away old clothes, books, furniture, etc. Give them to us! We can sell them and use the money to buy recycling bins, benches, trees, etc. for our neighborhood. We organize a garage sale every Saturday at a different place in the neighborhood. Check out our website.

Clean-up Sunday
Help us clean up the parks in the neighborhood. We need lots of volunteers to pick up trash, plant trees, put up benches, paint fences and old benches, etc. Meet us outside the Hillside Community Center every Sunday at 8 a.m.

E-cycling Day
Do you have old cell phones, gadgets or TVs? Well, it's not a good idea to throw them away. We can help you recycle them properly. Bring them to Hillside parking lot every Tuesday from 9 a.m. to 2 p.m.

Do you have old appliances, like refrigerators and washing machines? Well, don't worry. We can come and get them. Just call us!

Contact us at: 555-936-7141   www.greenneighborhood.net

B. Read again and answer the questions.

1. What does "Green Neighborhood" sell at garage sales?
2. When does "Green Neighborhood" organize them?
3. Where can you find information about garage sales?
4. What do volunteers do on Clean-up Sunday?
5. Where do volunteers meet?
6. What can you recycle on E-cycling Day?
7. When and where does "Green Neighborhood" organize E-cycling Day?

3 Grammar Object Personal Pronouns → *p. 113*

A. Read the examples. What do you notice about the words in blue?

> I want a croissant. Give **me** a croissant, please.
>
> **You** need help. I can help **you**.
>
> Tony's a volunteer. **He**'s nice. I like **him**.
>
> There's Diane. **She**'s new here. You know **her**, right?
>
> Look at that fence. **It**'s old. Let's paint **it**.
>
> **We** want information about *Green Neighborhood*. Tell **us** about it.
>
> I don't want these magazines. **They**'re old. Put **them** in the recycling bin.

B. Complete with object personal pronouns.

1. **A:** How do your children get to school?
   B: I drive _____ to school every day.

2. **A:** I love that cell phone.
   B: It's not very expensive. Buy _____.

3. **A:** Isn't Dave here today?
   B: No, he's sick. Call _____ at home.

4. **A:** I want to go bowling with you and your friends.
   B: OK, meet _____ at the subway station at 7 p.m.

5. **A:** Bring _____ my sunglasses, please.
   B: Here you are.

6. **A:** Where's Jenny?
   B: I don't know. I can't find _____.

4 Pronunciation 🔊

A. Listen and repeat. Notice the difference in pronunciation.

/ʃ/	tra**sh**	informa**ti**on	electri**ci**an
/s/	**s**ave	re**c**ycle	acro**ss**
/tʃ/	ben**ch**	**ch**eck	signa**t**ure

Pay attention to the spelling of words. Not all sounds have the same spelling.

B. Say these words and check the correct sound. Then listen and check your answers.

	trash /ʃ/	save /s/	bench /tʃ/
channel			
fini**sh**			
fen**c**e			
chef			
ti**ss**ues			
furni**t**ure			
web**s**ite			
station			

A. Think about your neighborhood and answer the questions below. You can keep notes if you like.

- How "green" is your neighborhood?
- What are the parks like? Are they clean? Do they have trees, recycling bins, trash cans, benches, etc.?
- What are the schools like?
- What are the streets like?
- How can you change your neighborhood to make it "greener?"
- What events can you organize to help?

B. Talk in groups of three. Discuss and decide what changes you would like to make to your neighborhood and what events you can organize.

> 66 *Let's clean up... park.*
> *That's a good idea. There's a lot of trash there.*
> *I think so, too. We can also...*
> *I don't think so. Maybe we can plant trees and...*
> *Of course. We can also...*
> *I'm not sure about that. Let's organize...* 99

C. Work in groups. Make a poster advertising your plans from activity B. Include the following information.

- place
- date
- activities
- contact information

D. Present your poster to the class.

1 Vocabulary 🔊

Match the sights with the phrases. Then listen and check your answers.
Which of these can be found in the town/city where you live? What are they called?

a. You can watch a game there.
b. You can see wild animals there.
c. You can buy things there.
d. You can watch a play there.
e. You can see fish and other water creatures there.
f. You can see important objects and paintings there.
g. You can see old buildings and learn about history there.

museum **1**

zoo **2**

theater **3**

market **4**

aquarium **5**

castle **6**

stadium **7**

2 Listening 🔊

Listen to four short dialogues. Where are the people? Match. There is one extra place you do not need to use.

> **TIP**
> Listen for key words to understand the main ideas.

Dialogue 1	at a stadium
Dialogue 2	at an aquarium
Dialogue 3	at a castle
Dialogue 4	at a theater
	at a museum

3 Writing A description of one's town/city

A. Read the text and answer the question.

Where can you find a text like this?
a. in a letter **b.** in a brochure **c.** in an encyclopedia

Beautiful Barcelona!

What to see

Barcelona is famous for its architecture. There are lots of buildings by the famous architect Antoni Gaudi. Go downtown to see them.

There are over 55 museums in the city so there are lots of things to see. Also, don't miss Montjuic Castle. Visit it and learn about the history of Catalonia.

Remember to visit the Camp Nou Stadium. It is famous because it is the home of FC Barcelona.

What to do

Barcelona has fantastic places to walk around, like Park Guell. Also, go to La Rambla. This beautiful street has restaurants, coffee shops and lots of stores.

Don't forget to visit one of the seven beaches, like Barceloneta beach. They are very popular. Go swimming or just go for a walk.

How to get around

There are buses, trams and an excellent subway system. The best way to see Barcelona is to walk around or rent a bicycle or a scooter. There are lots of bicycle lanes in the city.

B. Read again. Can you name the places in the pictures?

C. Read the note below and find what the highlighted words 1-4 in the text on the left refer to.

Avoiding repetition

When writing, try not to repeat the same words all the time. Use:

• he/she/it/we/they (subject personal pronouns)

Lots of **children** visit the zoo. ~~The children~~ *They* love the animals.

• him/her/it/us/them (object personal pronouns)

The market has lots of things to buy. Don't miss ~~the market~~ *it*.

1. them: _____

2. it: _____

3. it: _____

4. They: _____

D. Think about your town/city. In groups, discuss the following questions. Then look at the table below and write down some notes.

• What are some popular sights in your town/city?
• Where are they?
• Do you know anything about them?
• Do a lot of people visit them?

• What can tourists do in your town/city?
• Where is a good place to go shopping?

• How can people get around your town/city?
• What is the best way to see the town/city?

66 ... *has lots of museums.*

That's right, and I think The National Museum is very popular.

Yes, lots of tourists visit it. There's also the... **99**

What to see	What to do	How to get around

E. Write a few paragraphs describing your town/city. Use the headings and your notes from activity D. Also, use the phrases given below.

In... there is/are...	Walk around...
... has..., like the...	Remember to...
The... is very famous/popular.	Don't forget to...
The best way to see... is to...	Don't miss...
Go to / Visit...	

Vocabulary

A. Circle the correct words.

1. The movie theater isn't **near / far**. Let's walk there.

2. Please, **pick / put** up your clothes from the floor.

3. They need lots of **volunteers / tourists** to clean the beach. Do you want to go?

4. It is **popular / important** to protect the environment.

5. The coffee shop is **across / between** from a Chinese restaurant.

6. The **castle / hotel** is open from 9 a.m. to 5 p.m.

B. Complete with the words in the box.

transportation	paintings	aquarium
plant	lot	traffic

1. There are lots of _____ by Picasso in that museum.

2. Do you use public _____ to get to work?

3. There's a big parking _____ behind the supermarket.

4. Turn left at the _____ lights.

5. The _____ is awesome. Visit it.

6. Let's _____ trees around the school.

Grammar

C. Complete with *can* and the words in parentheses. Give short answers where possible.

1. **A:** _____ (Mary / cook)?

   B: Of course, _____. She's a chef!

2. **A:** _____ (you / drive) a car?

   B: No, _____, but I _____ (ride) a motorcycle.

3. **A:** Nancy _____ (use) a computer pretty well.

   B: Really? She's only seven years old. _____ (she / send) e-mails, too?

   A: Yes, _____.

   B: Wow!

D. Complete with object personal pronouns.

1. Those newspapers are old. Let's recycle _____.

2. My grandmother is sick and I want to visit _____.

3. There's a documentary about colleges on TV this evening. Don't miss _____.

4. Where's Mr. Bean? I want to speak to _____.

5. Don't go out alone. Wait for _____. We want to come, too.

6. I'm late. Give _____ a ride to the subway station, please.

E. Rewrite using *Don't* and the words given.

1. Turn left at the bank. | right |

   _____

2. Remember to call Peter. | forget |

   _____

3. Go to bed early. | late |

   _____

4. Throw trash in trash cans. | in the street |

   _____

Communication

F. Complete the dialogues with the sentences.

> **a.** It's about a 10-minute walk.
> **b.** Where's the theater?
> **c.** Go straight.
> **d.** How do I get there?
> **e.** Go down Elwood Avenue and turn right at the supermarket.

A: Excuse me. **1** _____

B: It's across from the police station.

A: Where's that? Is it far?

B: No, it's isn't. **2** _____

A: Great. **3** _____

B: Go down this road and turn right at the museum. **4** _____ Then turn left at the traffic lights. That's Elwood Avenue. **5** _____ The theater is on your left.

A: Thank you.

> **f.** The best way is to take a taxi.
> **g.** What is there to see in this town?
> **h.** No problem.
> **i.** I think so.

A: Excuse me. **6** _____

B: Well, there's the Modern Art Museum and the zoo.

A: A zoo? Is it open today?

B: **7** _____

A: Great. How can I get there?

B: Well, it's far. **8** _____

A: OK, thanks.

B: **9** _____

Self-assessment

Read the following and check the appropriate boxes. For the points you are unsure of, refer back to the relevant sections in the module.

now i can...

) talk about the modes of transportation I use	☐
) talk about my abilities	☐
) refer to the location of places in a town/city	☐
) read a map	☐
) ask for, give and follow directions	☐
) express my opinion	☐
) talk about places in my town/city	☐
) avoid repetition when writing	☐
) write a description of my town/city	☐

Discuss:

- Label the pictures using the words in the box. Are these words similar in your language?

| tomato | pizza | sandwich |
| salad | chocolate | soup |

- What's your favorite food?

- Where do you usually go when you eat out?

In this module you will learn...

- to talk about food preferences

- to ask and answer about quantity

- to make, accept and refuse an offer

- to read a menu

- to order food and drink

- to create, conduct and report the results of a survey

- to use linking words (and, but, or)

- to talk and write about eating habits

1 Vocabulary 🔊

Listen. What other kinds of food can you add to these categories?

fruit

orange · apple · bananas

strawberries · pineapple

vegetables

carrots · potato · onions

lettuce · cucumbers

dairy products

milk · cheese · yogurt

meat

chicken · lamb · beef

grain products

rice · bread · pasta

2 Reading 🔊

A. Look at the title of the text below. Do you know what a vegetarian and a meat eater eats? Listen, read and check your answers.

Vegetarian or

I'm a vegetarian, so I don't eat meat or fish. I eat dairy products and eggs, and of course I love all kinds of vegetables, especially tomatoes. I even have some tomato plants in my garden. For a snack, I usually have an egg sandwich and some tomato juice. It's delicious. I don't eat fruit very often and I can't stand strawberries or bananas.

Betty, 23

Meat eater?

I love meat and I eat some every day! My favorite is beef and I usually have a steak with some rice. I don't like vegetables very much, but I try to have a salad with every meal, because vegetables are good for you. I love all kinds of fruit and fruit juices. My favorite is apple and strawberry. However, I hate one thing and that's eggs! I can't eat them.

Stuart, 29

B. Read again and answer the questions.

1. Who likes vegetables?

2. Who eats vegetables?

3. What does Betty have in her garden?

4. What does Betty have with her sandwich?

5. Who can't stand eggs?

6. What does Stuart eat with rice?

7. Who likes fruit?

8. What fruit does Betty never eat?

9. What is in Stuart's favorite juice?

3 Grammar Countable and uncountable nouns, a(n) - some → *p. 114*

A. Read the examples and match.

1. There's **a sandwich** on the table. ☐
2. There's **some bread** in the bag. ☐
3. There are **some carrots** in the refrigerator. ☐

a. some + plural countable nouns

b. a(n) + singular countable nouns

c. some + uncountable nouns

B. Complete with *a*, *an* or *some*.

1. **A:** Let's make a fruit salad. There are _____ apples and _____ strawberries in the refrigerator.

   B: Here's _____ banana and _____ orange.

   A: Great. Let's put _____ yogurt, too.

2. **A:** I have _____ vegetable soup and _____ bread for lunch. What do you have?

   B: I have _____ salad and _____ cheese.

   A: Here's _____ bread, too.

   B: Thanks.

3. Let's go to the supermarket. We need _____ onions and _____ potatoes.

4 Pronunciation 🔊

A. Listen and repeat. Notice the difference in pronunciation.

/g/	e**gg**	**g**arden
/dʒ/	oran**ge**	**j**uice

B. Say the words below. In which category do they belong? Listen and check your answers.

yo**g**urt   ve**g**etables   refri**g**erator   **g**rocery

ma**g**azine   **g**ym   ve**g**etarian   colle**g**e   collea**g**ue

5 Speaking & Writing

A. Talk in pairs about your food preferences and eating habits. Discuss the questions below.

- Are you a vegetarian?
- Are you a meat eater?
- Do you like fruit and vegetables?
- What's your favorite fruit/vegetable?
- What do you usually eat for a snack?
- What do you usually have with meat or fish?
- What do you hate?

❝ *I don't like vegetables at all. What about you?*

I like all kinds of vegetables, especially lettuce. ❞

B. Write a few sentences about your food preferences and eating habits. Use your ideas from activity A above.

6b

1 Vocabulary 🔊

Listen. Which of the following kinds of food and drink do you like and which don't you like?

apple pie | ice cream

cake | tea | taco | tuna | soda

mayonnaise | (French) fries | ketchup | mustard | pepper | chicken nuggets | salt | mushrooms | onion rings

2 Reading 🔊

A. Listen and read. What do the two women order? Choose a or b.

1. A: Next please.

B: What kind of sandwiches do you have?

A: Tuna, chicken, and egg.

B: What's in the egg sandwich?

A: Egg, mayonnaise, lettuce and tomatoes.

B: I'd like an egg sandwich and some... No wait! I want a tuna sandwich without any onions.

A: Is that all?

B: And some fries.

A: Small, medium or large?

B: Large, please.

A: Would you like some ketchup with your fries?

B: No, thank you, but I'd like some extra salt.

A: Sure. Anything to drink?

B: No, thanks.

2. C: Are you ready to order?

D: Yes. Do you have any sandwiches?

C: No, I'm afraid we don't have any sandwiches.

D: No problem. Umm... I'd like a cappuccino, please.

C: Sugar?

D: No, thank you, but I'd like some cinnamon.

C: Sure. Anything else?

D: That apple pie looks good. I'd like some of that, too, with some vanilla ice cream.

C: Certainly.

3 Grammar some / any → p. 114

A. Read the examples. In which cases do we use *some* and *any*?

There's **some** cake on the table.
There are **some** tacos in the oven.
Would you like **some** tea?

There isn't **any** mustard in this sandwich.
Do you have **any** chicken nuggets?

B. Complete with *some* or *any*.

1. **A:** Would you like **1** _____ coffee?

   B: No, thanks.

   A: What about **2** _____ apple pie?

   B: Yes, please. Do you have **3** _____ ice cream to go with it?

   A: No, I'm afraid I don't.

2. **A:** There isn't **4** _____ salt on these fries.

   B: Here you are. Do you want **5** _____ ketchup?

   A: No, thanks. Do you have **6** _____ mayonnaise?

   B: For your fries?

   A: No, I want **7** _____ for my sandwich.

3. **A:** Would you like **8** _____ rice with your steak?

   B: No. Do you have **9** _____ onion rings?

   A: Of course. Anything else?

   B: **10** _____ tea, please, without **11** _____ sugar.

B. Read again and answer the questions. Write A-D. You will not need to use all the letters.

1. Who is a customer? ☐ + ☐

2. Who doesn't order anything to drink? ☐

3. Who orders dessert? ☐

4. Who changes her order? ☐

5. Who can't have what she wants? ☐

We use **want** and **would like** (+ noun **or** to + base form of verb) to say what we want and to make offers and requests.
I'd like to order, please.
Do you want some tea?
Would you like to try some cake?

4 Listening 🔊

Listen to two people ordering and look at the menu below. Write M for Man and W for Woman next to what they order.

Jerry's Place

SNACKS

tacos ☐
chicken nuggets ☐
fries ☐
onion rings ☐

SANDWICHES

chicken and tomato ☐
cheese and cucumber ☐
tuna and mushroom ☐

DRINKS

tea ☐
coffee ☐
mineral water ☐
soda ☐
fresh fruit juice: orange ☐
pineapple ☐

DESSERTS

ice cream: vanilla ☐
chocolate ☐
banana ☐
strawberry ☐
carrot cake ☐
apple pie ☐

5 Speaking Role play
Talk in pairs.

Student A: Imagine you are a waiter/waitress at JERRY'S PLACE above. Look at the menu and cross out three items. Then take Student B's order. Use the phrases in the box.

Are you ready to order?
Would you like to order?
I'm afraid we don't have any...
Would you like... with that?
What would you like to drink / for dessert?
Anything to drink with that?
Small, medium or large?
Anything else?
Is that all?
Certainly.

Student B: Imagine you are a customer at JERRY'S PLACE and you want to order. Student A is the waiter/waitress. Give him/her your order. Use the phrases in the box.

Excuse me, I'd like to order.
I'd like..., please.
I don't want any... / I want... without any...
Yes, please. / No, thank you.
Do you have...?
Is there any...?
What's in the...?
No, that's all.

1 Reading 🔊

A. Listen and read. How many questions does the woman ask Mrs. Pickles?

MRS. PICKLES

Excuse me, I'd like to ask you some questions for a survey.

Well, I'm late for my doctor's appointment. How many questions?

Umm... Just one or two. It's a survey about healthy eating.

Oh, all right. I'm a very healthy eater, you know. I don't eat a lot of junk food.

I'm sure. How many cups of coffee do you have a day?

Just one cup.

OK, and how much fruit do you eat?

Oh, a lot. Mostly lemons.

Lemons?

Yes, I eat some lemon pie every day. I sometimes have apple pie, or strawberry cheesecake. They all have fruit in them, right?

I guess. Umm... What snacks do you have when you're hungry?

I'm hungry now. And that's your third question. So bye! I'm a busy woman.

Now, where can I get some lemon pie?

B. Read again and write T for True or F for False.

1. The woman asks Mrs. Pickles about her eating habits. ☐

2. Mrs. Pickles has a small cup of coffee every day. ☐

3. Mrs. Pickles doesn't eat a lot of desserts. ☐

4. Mrs. Pickles doesn't answer the woman's last question. ☐

5. Mrs. Pickles is hungry after the survey. ☐

2 Vocabulary 🔊

Listen. Can you think of any more examples?

a bottle of water   **a glass of milk**   **a cup of hot chocolate**   **a can of tomato sauce**

a slice of cake   **a box of cookies**   **a bag of chips**

a bar of chocolate

> We say **a bar of chocolate** or **a chocolate bar**.

3 Grammar How much? / How many?
→ p. 114

A. Read the examples and look at the phrases in blue. Which phrase do we use with countable nouns and which with uncountable nouns?

> **A:** How much water do you want?
> **B:** I want a lot. Get me a big glass, please. I'm thirsty.
>
> **A:** How many cookies are there in the box?
> **B:** Ten, I think.

B. Complete with *how much* or *how many*.

1. A: _____ slices of tomato do you want in your sandwich?

   B: Just two. _____ cheese do we have?

   A: We have lots of cheese. _____ slices do you want?

   B: Two. And some mustard, please.

2. A: Let's make some pasta. I'm hungry.

   B: Me too. _____ bags of pasta do we need?

   A: Just one. There are only two of us. And we need some mushrooms and...

   B: _____ cans? Two?

   A: Yes. And some tomatoes for the sauce.

   B: We don't have any.

   A: Oh, do we have any ketchup?

   B: Yes. _____ ketchup do we need? Is one bottle OK?

   A: Yes, that's fine.

Task

A. Listen to four people answering questions for a survey. Which question are they answering? Match the speakers with the questions a-d below. 🔊

Kelly ☐   Debbie ☐   Robert ☐   Simon ☐

a. How much water do you drink a day?

b. How many bags of chips do you eat a week?

c. How much coffee do you drink a day?

d. How many cookies do you eat a week?

B. Create a survey. Write the questions using *How much / How many* and the prompts given.

- cans of soda / drink / a week?
- bottles of water / drink / a day?
- fruit / eat / a day?
- eggs / eat / a week?
- milk / drink / a day?
- chocolate / eat / a week?

SURVEY: HEALTHY EATING HABITS

How many	

C. Work in groups of three, asking two questions each from the survey above. Note down your classmates' answers in the space next to the questions.

D. Report the results of the survey to the class.

> 66 *One student in my group drinks lots of soda. He drinks about ten cans a week.* 99

1 Vocabulary 🔊

Listen. Do you ever have any of these for breakfast, lunch or dinner?

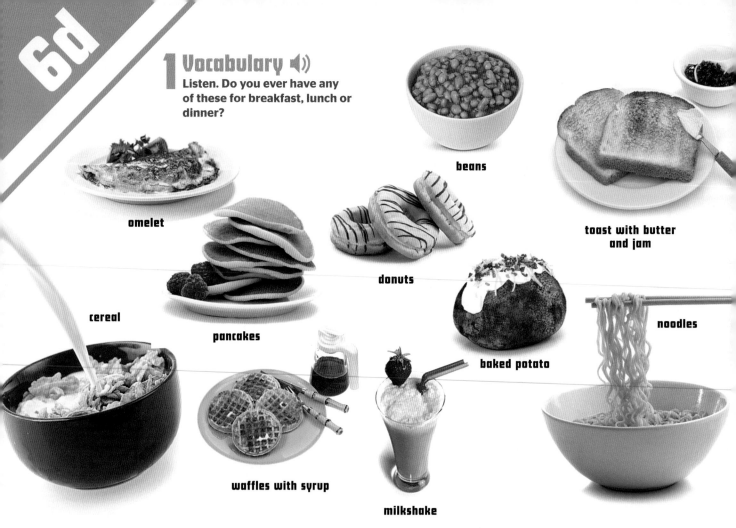

omelet

cereal

pancakes

donuts

waffles with syrup

milkshake

beans

toast with butter and jam

baked potato

noodles

2 Listening 🔊

Listen to two short dialogues and answer the questions. Choose picture a, b or c.

1. What does Ian usually have for breakfast?

a

b

c

2. Where does the woman go every Friday night?

a Traditional ITALIAN restaurant

b MEXICAN RESTAURANT

c HUNGARIAN CUISINE

3 Speaking

A. Discuss.

• Do you like food from other countries?
• What types of restaurants are there in your town/city?
• What kind of food do they have?
• Do you often go to these restaurants?
• Do you order out from these restaurants?

66 *I really like Chinese, Italian and Mexican food. There are lots of restaurants... Chinese restaurants have noodles...* 99

B. Think about your favorite restaurant and complete the table below. Then in pairs, talk about your favorite restaurant and give each other information about it.

NAME	_____
TYPE	_____
ADDRESS	_____
	_____
FAVORITE DISH	_____

66 *What's the name of the restaurant?*
    ...
What type of restaurant is it?
    ... 99

4 Writing A short text about eating habits

A. Read the text below. What is the main topic of each paragraph?

Full English Breakfast

In the U.K., breakfast is a very important meal. The traditional English breakfast includes fried eggs, fried tomatoes, mushrooms, baked beans, toast, potato patties called hash browns, and tea or coffee. Not many British people eat it during the week.

I never have time to cook in the morning before work, but I never skip breakfast. I usually have cereal and two slices of toast with jam. I don't drink coffee at home, but I always have a glass of orange juice or pineapple juice. My breakfast isn't very big, but it helps me start my busy day.

See also:

B. Read the note and complete the sentences 1-6 with *and*, *but* or *or*.

Linking words

- We use **and** to join similar ideas.
  For dinner, I have a salad.
  For dinner, I also have a yogurt.
  For dinner, I have a salad **and** a yogurt.

- We use **but** to join two opposite ideas.
  I like butter.
  I don't like jam.
  I like butter, **but** I don't like jam.
  I don't like jam, **but** I like butter.

- We use **or** to show that there is a choice or alternative.
  Do you want pancakes?
  Do you want waffles?
  Do you want pancakes **or** waffles?

1. For lunch, I have a sandwich _____ a baked potato, not both.

2. My friends don't usually have breakfast, _____ I do.

3. I always put mushrooms _____ lots of cheese in my omelet.

4. I eat lots of fruit, _____ I don't eat vegetables.

5. I love pancakes with butter, syrup _____ strawberries.

6. At the office, we sometimes order Chinese _____ Mexican.

MEAL:	
People in my country	
Me	

C. Think of people's eating habits in your country. Choose a meal (breakfast, lunch or dinner) and in pairs, discuss some of the following questions. Then write down some notes in the red table above.

People in my country
What do people in your country usually have for this meal?
What else does this meal include?
What time do they have it?
How big is this meal?
Do they drink anything with this meal?
Where do they usually eat this meal?
Who do they usually eat this meal with?

D. In pairs, discuss some of the following questions about your eating habits. Then write down some notes in the red table above.

Me
What do you usually have for this meal?
What time do you have it?
How big is this meal?
Do you drink anything with this meal?
Where do you usually eat this meal?
Who do you usually eat with?

E. Write about the meal you have chosen in activities C and D, using your notes. Write a paragraph describing people's eating habits in your country and another paragraph describing your eating habits.

> **TIP**
> When writing, link your ideas so that your writing flows. Use *and, but, or.*

Vocabulary

A. Put the words in the correct category.

donut butter beef cucumber rice pineapple
cheesecake strawberries cheese bread
chicken onion apple pie yogurt pasta
orange lettuce lamb

fruit	vegetables

dairy products	grain products

meat	desserts

B. Circle the correct words.

1. This milkshake is **delicious / traditional**! Have some.

2. I'd like some fries without any **sugar / salt**.

3. We're really **healthy / hungry**. What's for lunch?

4. I have two chocolate **bars / slices**. Do you want one?

5. It's good to eat five small **meals / juices** a day.

6. There's a **can / bottle** of water in the refrigerator.

Grammar

C. Complete with *a(n)*, *some* or *any*.

1. **A:** Is there _____ ice cream in the refrigerator?

   B: Of course. Let's make _____ milkshake. There are _____ strawberries and here's _____ banana.

   A: Good idea. Bring me _____ milk, too, please.

2. **A:** I usually have _____ omelet and _____ cereal for breakfast. What about you?

   B: I don't have breakfast. I usually get up late, drink _____ coffee and go to work.

D. Complete with *how much* or *how many*.

1. **A:** _____ eggs do we need for the cake?

   B: Three, I think.

   A: And _____ milk?

   B: Just a glass.

2. **A:** _____ mayonnaise do you want in your sandwich?

   B: I don't want any, but I'd like some cheese.

   A: _____ cheese?

   B: Two slices, please.

Communication

E. Match.

1. Are you ready to order? ☐
2. Is that all, then? ☐
3. What's in the vegetable soup? ☐
4. Anything to drink with that? ☐
5. What do you usually have for dinner? ☐
6. Would you like an omelet or a steak? ☐
7. I'd like some pancakes with syrup, please. ☐

a. Potato, carrots and some mushrooms.

b. Yes, I'd like two tacos, please.

c. Both. I'm very hungry.

d. No, I'd like some cheesecake, too.

e. A salad.

f. No, thank you.

g. I'm afraid we don't have any.

F. Put the dialogue in order.

☐ Yes, please. I'd like some chocolate cake.

☐ Certainly, what would you like?

☐ What about some dessert?

☐ No, thank you.

☐ A tuna sandwich and some fries.

1 Excuse me, I'd like to order.

☐ Would you like some ketchup with that?

Self-assessment

Read the following and check the appropriate boxes. For the points you are unsure of, refer back to the relevant sections in the module.

NOW I CAN...

- ❯ talk about food preferences ☐
- ❯ ask and answer about quantity ☐
- ❯ make, accept and refuse an offer ☐
- ❯ read a menu ☐
- ❯ order food and drink ☐
- ❯ use linking words (and, but, or) ☐
- ❯ talk and write about eating habits ☐

How's it going?

Pretty good. 😊 And you?

chat on the Net

check the news/ weather

NEWS

download information/ songs/movies

Discuss:
- Do you have a PC, laptop or tablet?
- What do you use it for?
- Do you surf the Net? What for?

play video games

check e-mail

work/study

Online 7

In this module you will learn...

- to talk about things that are happening now
- expressions used when making a phone call
- useful language related to computers
- to ask for help and offer help
- to give thanks and respond to thanks
- to write facts for a quiz
- to talk about the weather
- to make suggestions
- to write a letter/e-mail to a friend

1 Reading 🔊

A. Read the dialogues and put them in the correct order. Then listen and check your answers.

a ☐

Woman Henderson's Flowers, how may I help you?

Steve Hello, I'm trying to order from your website but it isn't working.

Woman I'm sorry, sir. Would you like to order over the phone?

Steve Yes, please... Hold on... I'm looking at the flowers on the site now. Yes, I'd like the Spring yellow flowers. The number is 96751.

Woman Certainly. Would you like us to send them to your home?

Steve No, they're for my sister. Lucy Collins, 234 Bridge Street.

b ☐

Steve Oh, I can't do it.

Mark What's up, Steve?

Steve I'm trying to order some flowers from Henderson's but their website isn't working.

Mark Maybe your tablet has a problem. Use my laptop.

Steve No, my tablet's fine.

Mark Who are the flowers for?

Steve It's Lucy's graduation tomorrow, remember?

Mark Of course, I do. She's my sister, too, you know.

Steve What's that? Is that Lucy on Skype?

Mark Yep.

Steve Don't tell her about the flowers.

c ☐

Mark Hi, Lucy!

Lucy Hi, Mark! Are you ready for tomorrow?

Mark What's tomorrow?

Lucy My graduation!

Mark I know, I'm just kidding.

Lucy Is Steve there? He isn't answering his cell.

Steve I'm here, Lucy. I think my cell's in my car. Listen, I can't talk right now. Call me back later. I need to make a phone call. Bye!

B. Read the dialogues again and match to make true sentences.

Lucy

Steve

Mark

is using a tablet.

wants to order some flowers.

's graduation is tomorrow.

calls a flower store.

has a laptop.

is skyping the others.

2 Vocabulary 🔊

Listen. How do you communicate with family and friends?

talk on the phone

send text messages

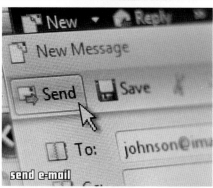

send e-mail

use social media sites / instant messaging

use Skype

3 Grammar Present Progressive (affirmative - negative)

→ p. 114

A. Read the examples. These actions are happening now. What do you notice about the formation of the Present Progressive?

> Ryan **is driving** to work. He **isn't taking** the bus today.
> Emma and Anna **aren't eating** lunch. They **are having** coffee.

B. Complete with the Present Progressive of the verbs in parentheses.

1. Justin _____ (not read) a book. He _____ (surf) the Net.

2. Helen and Sally _____ (not study). They _____ (play) a video game.

3. Connor _____ (chat) with his friends on the Net and his brother _____ (watch) the news.

4. Alex _____ (not talk) on the phone. He _____ (send) a text message.

5. Brian _____ (try) to skype his parents, but it _____ (not work).

4 Pronunciation 🔊

A. Listen and repeat. Notice the difference in pronunciation.

/n/	liste**n**
/ŋ/	listeni**ng**

B. Say the words below. In which category do they belong? Listen and check your answers.

song   walki**ng**   kitche**n**   studyi**ng**   pho**n**e   spri**ng**

graduatio**n**   kiddi**ng**

5 Speaking Role play

Talk in pairs.

Student A: Imagine you are friends with Student B's brother, Tim, and you call him at home. Student B answers the phone. Ask for your friend.

Student B: Imagine you are at home and your brother, Tim, is busy. Student A calls and wants to speak to him. Talk to Student A as in the example.

❝ *Hello?*
   Hello, is Tim there, please?
Yes, but he can't talk right now. He's...
   Can I leave a message?
Sure.
   I'm ..., by the way. Tell him that... ❞

1 Reading 🔊
Listen, read and answer the questions. Write A-F.

1.
A: Hi, Julie. What are you doing?
B: I'm surfing the Net.
A: What are you looking for?
B: Information about Art Colleges, but I can't find much.
A: Need any help?
B: Sure, thanks. That's very kind of you.
A: No problem. I know a good site. You can download lots of information about colleges in our area. Let me show you.

2.
C: Excuse me, can you help me?
D: What can I do for you? Are you having trouble with the printer?
C: Yes, I'm trying to print my assignment but it isn't working. I press this button but nothing happens. See?
D: I think the paper's stuck, but I don't know how to open this printer. Let me call a technician.
C: I can't wait. Thanks anyway.

3.
E: Hey, Terry. Are you leaving?
F: Yes.
E: Can you give me a hand here? I'm trying to install a program but I can't.
F: Sorry, but I'm late for an appointment.
E: Please!
F: Listen, I can help you tomorrow, first thing in the morning.
E: OK, see you tomorrow.

1. Who wants to help but doesn't know how? ☐
2. Who asks someone for help? ☐ ☐
3. Who helps someone else? ☐
4. Who is trying to find something on the Net? ☐
5. Who can help, but doesn't? ☐

2 Vocabulary 🔊
Listen. Then add the words in the box to the correct category. Can you think of anything else to add?

| your username | ENTER | antivirus software |
| a battery | the TV | a movie |

turn on/off a computer, _____

press a button, _____

install a program, _____

download information, _____

charge a cell phone, _____

enter a password, _____

3 Grammar Present Progressive (questions) → *p. 114*

A. Read the examples. How is the question formed?

> What **is Harriet doing** right now?
> She's watching TV.
>
> **Are Ollie and Fred studying** right now? → Yes, they are.
> → No, they aren't.

B. Complete the sentences with the Present Progressive of the verbs in parentheses.

1. A: _____ you _____ (read) the newspaper?

   B: Yes, I am. Actually, I _____ (look) for a new apartment.

2. A: What _____ John _____ (do)?

   B: He _____ (download) some information for a school assignment.

3. A: _____ the children _____ (play) video games again?

   B: No, they aren't. They _____ (try) to install an antivirus program on their new laptop.

4 Listening ◀))

Listen to two short dialogues and answer the questions.

1.

a. What is Ken trying to do?

_____

b. What does Richard tell him to do first?

_____

2.

a. What is Natalie doing?

_____

b. Does Jenny help her?

_____

5 Speaking

Talk in pairs. Use the ideas below and make up conversations, using the phrases in the boxes and the situations given.

Student A	Student B
Imagine you are at the college library and see your friend (Student B). Greet him/her and ask what he/she is doing.	
	Greet Student A and tell him/her what you're doing.
Ask him/her how it is going.	
	Answer and explain your problem. (You can use the ideas given or your own.) If you want, ask for some help.
Offer to help Student B.	
	Thank your friend.
Respond.	

Offering help	**Asking for help**	**Thanking**	**Responding to thanks**
Would you like some help?	Can you help me?	Thanks a lot.	No problem.
Do you need any help?	I need some help here.	That's very kind of you.	Don't mention it.
Need any help?	Can you give me a hand?	Thank you so much.	You're welcome.
What can I do for you?		That's OK. Thanks anyway.	
Can I give you a hand?			
Let me help you.			
How may I help you?			

Situations for Student B

- You are looking for information about Russia on the Net, but you can't find what you want.
- You are trying to turn on a laptop, but you don't know which button to press.
- You are trying to download a program on your tablet, but you can't do it.
- You are trying to enter a website, but you can't remember your password.
- You are surfing the Net to find a part-time job in your area, but you can't find any.
- You are trying to print your assignment, but the printer isn't working.

1 Vocabulary ◀))

Match the icons with the actions. Then listen and check your answers.

1 **2** **3** **4** **5** **6** **7**

a. cut   **b.** copy   **c.** paste   **d.** delete   **e.** save   **f.** print   **g.** open

2 Reading ◀))

A. What happens when you press the following keys on a keyboard? Listen, read and check your answers.

Ctrl + O   Ctrl + F   Ctrl + C

Keyboard shortcuts

Keyboard shortcuts are very useful because instead of using your mouse and clicking on a lot of buttons, you just press one or two keys to open a file, print a document, etc.

At the top of the keyboard there are "function" keys. These are shortcut keys and have the letter F with a number, for example F1. This key almost always opens the "help" section of a program.

Some useful keyboard shortcuts use two keys together, like Ctrl+C for "copy" and Ctrl+F for "find." For these simple shortcuts, you just need to know the first letter of the action, for example, Ctrl+P for "print", Ctrl+O for "open" and so on. English speakers are lucky because keyboard shortcuts are the same all over the world and don't change in other languages. For non-English speakers this can be confusing.

However, other shortcuts aren't so easy, like Ctrl+V for "paste." Computer users remember this because it is like an arrow pointing down "onto" a document, but it's also the key next to "C" for "copy."

> Shortcuts are good because you don't use your mouse a lot. Using a mouse for many hours can injure the muscles in your hand.

> Try these keyboard shortcuts to see what they do:
> Ctrl+A
> Ctrl+S
> Ctrl+Esc

3 Intonation

A. Listen and repeat. Notice the syllable that is stressed in words *a* and *b*.

a. Internet   **b.** in**stead**

B. Read the following words and underline the stressed syllable. Then listen and check your answers.

computer   keyboard   document

technology   **useful**   protect

delete   remember   language

copy   confusing   **difficult**

B. Read again. What do the words in bold refer to?

1. You can use **these** instead of your mouse.
_____

2. These are at the top of your keyboard.
_____

3. You press **this** to open "help." _____

4. Some shortcuts use **this key** together with the first letter of the action. _____

5. This happens when you press Ctrl+P.
_____

6. These people have trouble remembering shortcuts. _____

7. This key is next to "V." _____

C. Look at the highlighted words/phrases in the text and choose the correct meaning *a* or *b*.

1. useful
   a. helping you do what you want
   b. easy to find

2. simple
   a. popular
   b. easy

3. confusing
   a. easy to understand
   b. difficult to understand

4. computer users
   a. people who use computers
   b. people who make computers

> **TIP**
> Try to guess the meaning of unknown words from the context.

A. Do the computer quiz below.

COMPUTER QUIZ

Task

1. Which country has the Internet country code .ch?
   a. China
   b. Switzerland
   c. Canada

2. What comes next after megabyte, gigabyte, terabyte...?
   a. petabyte
   b. ultrabyte
   c. zettabyte

3. Which institution usually has .edu at the end of its web address?
   a. a library
   b. a bank
   c. a college

4. What is QWERTY?
   a. a type of screen
   b. a type of keyboard
   c. a type of mouse

5. Which arrow is on the "ENTER" key?
   a. ↳ **b.** ↱
   c. ↵

B. Listen to a radio show revealing the answers to the quiz above. How many questions did you answer correctly?

C. Work in groups of four to make your own quiz. Try to come up with questions for a quiz about technology. Follow the guidelines below.

- Try to have questions on a variety of subjects:
  computers   cell phones   the Internet   video games
- If you need help with words, ask your teacher or use a dictionary.
- Remember to keep the answers to the quiz hidden on a separate piece of paper.

D. Hand out your quiz to different groups and see if they can answer the questions.

E. When your classmates have completed the quiz, reveal the answers.

1 Vocabulary 🔊

Listen. What's the weather like in your town/city today?

Paris 77ºF Monday — It's sunny.

Moscow 60ºF Monday — It's cloudy.

Melbourne 62ºF Monday — It's windy.

Seattle 28ºF Monday — It's snowing.

Jeddah 100ºF Monday — It's hot.

Kiev 23ºF Monday — It's cold.

Chicago 55ºF Monday — It's raining.

TIP
When you learn new words, you should remember if they are verbs, nouns, adjectives, etc.

2 Listening 🔊

Listen and answer the questions. Choose a, b or c.

1. What's the weather like in New York?
   a. It's raining.
   b. It's sunny.
   c. It's snowing.

2. What do the people decide to do?
   a. go out for dinner
   b. go to the movies
   c. stay home

3. What are the people doing?
   a. They are watching TV.
   b. They are reading a newspaper.
   c. They are surfing the Net.

3 Speaking

A. Discuss.

- Do you check the weather before you go out?
- What do you usually do on the weekend when the weather is good?
- What do you usually do on the weekend when the weather is bad?
- What's your favorite type of weather?

B. Talk in groups of three. Discuss, make suggestions and decide what to do. Use the ideas below and the weather words from activity 1, as in the example.

cycling   park   DVDs   bowling   zoo   lunch
tennis   gym   shopping   coffee   video games
movies   beach   walk

❝ Let's decide what to do today. How about going for a walk in the park?

No, it's cold and windy today.

Yeah. How about staying here and watching a DVD?

That's boring. How about going to the movies?

Nice idea!

OK, that sounds like fun. ❞

To make suggestions, use the following structures:
Let's go...
How about going...?

4 Writing A letter/e-mail to a friend

A. Read the e-mail below and answer the questions.

1. Who is writing the e-mail?
2. What's the weather like in her area?
3. What is she doing now?
4. Is she having a good time?
5. What is her roommate doing?
6. What does she suggest doing after the exams?

Hello Wendy,

How's it going? What's the weather like over there? It's raining here, and I'm stuck inside. I'm studying for a History exam, but I need a break so now I'm writing some e-mails to my old friends. My roommate doesn't have any more exams, and she's playing loud video games in the living room. Very annoying! Hey, let's meet up and do something after the exams, OK? You can come down and stay with us for a while. How about going to a baseball game or a concert? Think about it.

Anyway, that's all for now, because I need to study. Aargh!! College is pretty difficult, don't you think?

Write back soon,
Rose

B. Read the note and complete the e-mail with the words in the box.

Set phrases for letters and e-mails

When you write a letter or an e-mail to a friend, don't forget:

- to start with **Dear** or **Hi/Hello** + first name
  Dear Jody,   Hi Roy,   Hello Brenda,

- to use a set phrase.
  How are you?   How's it going?   How's life?
  I hope you're well.   I'm writing to tell you about...

- to end with a set phrase. Write your first name under this.
  Yours,   Your friend,   Love,   Bye for now,
  See you soon,   Take care,   Write back soon,

bye   Cliff   hi   well   how

Inbox (1)   12:56 PM

1 _____ Roger,

2 _____ are you?
I hope you're 3 _____. It's a beautiful sunny day today. I'm at the park and I'm writing this on my new cell phone. How about taking a break from studying and coming here for a while? Call me!

4 _____ for now,

5 _____

C. Talk in pairs. Imagine that you and your partner live in different neighborhoods/towns/cities and are talking on the phone. Use the questions below.

- Where are you right now?
- What's the weather like?
- What are you doing?
- Who are you with?
- What's he/she doing?
- Are you having a good time?
- How about... tonight or tomorrow?

D. Write an e-mail to a friend who lives in a different neighborhood/town/city. Use your ideas from activity C.

TIP
Remember to use appropriate phrases to start and end your e-mail.

75

Vocabulary

A. Match.

1.	make	a.	someone a hand
2.	have	b.	a good time
3.	give	c.	on the TV
4.	chat	d.	a phone call
5.	turn	e.	on the Net

B. Choose a, b or c.

1. First you _____ the document, then you paste it.
   a. copy   b. delete   c. enter

2. Before you close the program, it asks you to _____ the document.
   a. click   b. save   c. charge

3. Take some warm clothes, because it's _____ outside.
   a. hot   b. sunny   c. cold

4. Great! The paper is _____ in the printer.
   a. loud   b. annoying   c. stuck

5. I need to send a _____ message to my brother.
   a. phone   b. text   c. call

6. Oh no, it's _____ and I don't have an umbrella with me.
   a. snowing   b. windy   c. raining

7. Don't _____ that button! Call the technician first.
   a. press   b. leave   c. turn on

8. This text is very _____. I can't understand any of it.
   a. confusing   b. simple   c. useful

C. Complete the sentences with the words in the box.

password	install	useful	difficult
	battery	assignment	

1. I have a new antivirus program, but I don't know how to _____ it.

2. Ian, can you help me with this _____?

3. After your username, you need to enter your _____.

4. Mr. Dean's Math exams are usually very _____.

5. This website is _____ for finding old books.

6. I need a new _____ for my cell phone. My old one doesn't charge.

Grammar

D. Complete the dialogues with the Present Progressive of the verbs in parentheses.

1. A: Hey, Jackie. _____ (you / use) the laptop?
   B: Yes, I am. I _____ (write) an e-mail.
   A: Do you ever send e-mail to Mom and Dad?
   B: Actually, I _____ (send) an e-mail to them now.

2. A: Where _____ (Sally / go)?
   B: Shopping.
   A: But it _____ (rain) outside.
   B: No, it isn't.

3. A: Is Emily in the kitchen?
   B: Yes, she is.

A: Great. What's for lunch?
B: She _____ (not make) lunch.
   She _____ (work) on her assignment.
A: So, what _____ (we / have) for lunch?
B: I don't know. Let's cook together. Come on!

Communication

E. Complete the dialogues with the sentences in the box.

a. That's very kind of you.
b. Can I leave a message?
c. Hold on.
d. The problem is I can't make them work.
e. You're welcome.
f. What can I do for you?

1. A: Hello?
   B: Hello. Is Kevin there, please?
   A: **1** _____ I think he's in his room. Kevin!...
      No, he's not there.
   B: **2** _____
   A: Sure. What do you want me to tell him?
   B: Just tell him to call me at my brother's house.
      I'm Mike, by the way. Thank you.
   A: **3** _____

2. A: Hello, is that Jo Jo's Electronics Store?
   B: Yes, it is. **4** _____
   A: I have a new TV and DVD player from your store.
      5 _____
   B: Well, I can send a technician to your house today.
   A: Really? **6** _____
   B: No problem.

F. Reply to the phrases below using *Let's* or *How about*.

1. I want to go out for dinner tonight.
   _____

2. Oh no! It's raining.
   _____

3. My printer is really old.
   _____

4. My cell phone isn't working.
   _____

5. There's a basketball game on TV.
   _____

Self-assessment

Read the following and check the appropriate boxes. For the points you are unsure of, refer back to the relevant sections in the module.

NOW I CAN...	
) talk about things that are happening now	☐
) have a conversation on the phone	☐
) use language related to computers	☐
) ask for help and offer help	☐
) thank and respond to thanks	☐
) talk about the weather	☐
) make suggestions	☐
) write a letter/e-mail to a friend	☐

first day at school

Discuss:
- Do you remember any of the events in the pictures?
- What is your earliest memory?

first cell phone

first vacation

first best friend

first bike

In this module you will learn...

- to talk about past events/experiences
- to give reason
- to talk about famous people in history and their achievements
- how suffixes are used to form nouns that refer to people
- to collaborate with others and write a short biography
- to talk about accidents and respond to bad news
- linking words/phrases used when listing events in order
- to write about a bad day

first car

1 Reading 🔊
A. Listen and read. Who had fun yesterday?

Hi John,
I went into the city yesterday. I met Linda at a coffee shop in the mall on Tilsdale Avenue. I had a cup of tea and we shared a piece of delicious chocolate cake. 😄 Then we went shopping. I got a new purse and Linda bought a (really ugly) hat. She liked it a lot and wore it the whole time. Embarrassing 😲! Then Linda gave me a ride home. We had a nice day. I really enjoyed it.

Hello John,
How are you? I had a terrible day yesterday 😩. I drove into the city and I met Diane at a horrible little coffee shop in Tilsdale Mall. I had an expensive cappuccino 😖 and tried some chocolate cake. Then we went shopping. We walked around for ages. But at least I found a beautiful hat 😄. It's so cool. Later, I took Diane home. She lives on the other side of the city! Nightmare!

B. Read again and complete the paragraph with words from the texts.

1 _____, Diane and Linda went to a 2 _____ in Tilsdale Mall. Diane had 3 _____ and Linda had 4 _____. They both had some 5 _____. Then they went 6 _____. Diane bought 7 _____ and Linda bought 8 _____. Diane thinks it's 9 _____. Later, 10 _____ drove 11 _____ home.

2 Grammar Past Simple (affirmative) → p. 115

A. Read the tables. What do you notice about the formation of the Past Simple of regular verbs?

Regular Verbs	
I	
You	
He	(watch →) watched
She	(live →) lived
It	(study →) studied
We	(stop →) stopped
You	
They	

Irregular Verbs	
I	
You	
He	(do →) did
She	(make →) made
It	(see →) saw
We	
You	
They	

TIME EXPRESSIONS
• yesterday / yesterday afternoon, etc.
• last night / week / Monday, etc.
• two days / a week / three years, etc. ago

B. Find regular and irregular verbs in activity 1 to complete the tables below.

Regular verbs

share → _____

like → _____

enjoy → _____

try → _____

walk → _____

Irregular verbs

go → _____   wear → _____

meet → _____   give → _____

have → _____   drive → _____

get → _____   find → _____

buy → _____   take → _____

For a list of irregular verbs go to page 117.

C. Complete with the Past Simple of the verbs in parentheses.

1. I _____ (play) video games yesterday and then I _____ (talk) on the phone with my friends.

2. Timothy _____ (find) a wallet on the street and _____ (give) it to a police officer.

3. Yesterday evening, my friends and I _____ (cook) a very nice meal. We _____ (make) pasta.

4. After work, I _____ (stop) at a coffee shop and _____ (have) some coffee and ice cream.

5. Fiona _____ (see) *Best Buddies II* at the movie theater two days ago and she really _____ (enjoy) it.

3 Pronunciation 🔊

A. Listen and repeat. Notice the difference in pronunciation.

/t/	watched	asked
/d/	played	lived
/ɪd/	wanted	needed

B. Say these words and check the correct sound. Then listen and check your answers.

	/t/	/d/	/ɪd/
visited			
helped			
listened			
washed			
hated			
started			
looked			
tried			

4 Speaking

Talk in pairs about what you did yesterday morning, afternoon and evening.

66 *Yesterday morning, I got up early and studied for an exam. What about you?*

Well, in the morning, I went shopping at the new mall. 99

5 Writing

Write a short e-mail to a friend telling him/her what you did yesterday.

1 Vocabulary ◀))

A. Listen. What other subjects did you do at school?

Mathematics (Math)

History

Geography

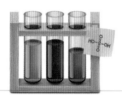

Chemistry

Physics

English Literature

IT (Information Technology)

Gym

Art

Biology

B. Look at the box and read the years a-e aloud. Listen and check your answers.

1996	nineteen ninety-six
2007	two thousand (and) seven
2012	twenty twelve

a. 2001
b. 1994
c. 2054
d. 1765
e. 1578

> in + year, century
> *I started college in 2003.*

2 Reading ◀))

A. Listen and read. What relationship do Ray and Julian have?

Julian Hey, you look familiar. Do I know you?

Ray I don't think so. I'm Ray.

Julian I'm Julian. By the way, did you go to Mayfield High?

Ray Yes, I did.

Julian I went there, too. I graduated in 2002.

Ray Me too. But I'm sorry, I don't remember you.

Julian I played on the football team. I had long hair back then.

Ray Julian Wilkins! Now, I remember. What a surprise! So, did you go to college?

Julian Yes, I did. I went to Starford College to study IT.

Ray IT? I thought you wanted to be an artist.

Julian Yeah, I did. I loved Art, but I didn't major in Art.

Ray And why did you choose to study IT?

Julian I chose IT because I also liked computers. So, I became a computer programmer. There are more chances of getting a job.

Ray And, did you find a job?

Julian Yeah, I got a job at *MultiTech* two years ago.

Ray *MultiTech*? My cousin, Mark Taylor, works there. Do you know Mark?

Julian Yeah, I work with him.

Ray Really? It's a small world.

> We use **Why...?** to ask about the reason why something happens.
> We use **because** to give the reason.
> *A: Why are you late?*
> *B: Because I got up late.*

B. Read again and write T for True or F for False.

1. Julian talked to Ray because he looked familiar. ☐
2. Ray went to Mayfield High, but Julian didn't. ☐
3. Julian had long hair at school. ☐
4. Julian studied both art and IT at college. ☐
5. Julian always wanted to be a computer programmer. ☐
6. Julian has a job. ☐
7. Ray is Mark's cousin. ☐

3 Grammar Past Simple (negative - questions) → p. 115

A. Read the examples. Which verb do you use to form the negative and question form?

> I **didn't go** to college. I got a job right after high school.
>
> Mr. Lambert **didn't teach** English. He taught French.
>
> When **did you talk** to Ronnie? Last night.
>
> **Did Paul walk** to work? ⟨ **Yes, he did.** / **No, he didn't.**

B. Complete the dialogues with the Past Simple of the verbs in parentheses.

1. **A:** Which college _____ John _____ (go) to?

   B: He _____ (go) to UCLA.

   A: _____ he _____ (major) in Math?

   B: Yes, he did.

   A: What year _____ he _____ (graduate)?

   B: He _____ (graduate) in 2010.

2. **A:** Why _____ you _____ (call) me last night?

   B: Because I _____ (need) Glen's e-mail address.

   A: _____ you _____ (find) it?

   B: No, I didn't.

   A: I'm really sorry, but I _____ (not call) you back because I _____ (have) work to do.

3. **A:** Do you remember Mrs. Stracina?

   B: _____ she _____ (teach) English Literature?

   A: No, she didn't. She _____ (teach) Geography.

   B: I _____ (not have) her for Geography. That's why I don't remember her.

4 Listening ◄))

Listen to three short dialogues and answer the questions. Choose a, b or c.

1. When did Tony graduate from school?
   - **a.** in 1998
   - **b.** in 1994
   - **c.** in 1999

2. Why did Dora major in History?
   - **a.** Because her mom is a History teacher, too.
   - **b.** Because she had a good teacher.
   - **c.** Because she wants to become a History teacher.

3. Which class did the two men have together?
   - **a.** Math
   - **b.** Art
   - **c.** Geography

5 Speaking

Talk in pairs. Use the prompts to ask each other questions about your school years.

- Which / school / go to?
- Which / subjects / like?
- like / Math?
- Why? / Why not?
- What year / graduate / from school?

- go / college?
- Which / college / go to?
- What / major in?
- Why / choose / that?
- When / graduate?

❝ *Which school did you go to?*
I went to... **❞**

A. Look at the books below and the title of the text. What do you know about the Brontë sisters and their books? Listen, read and find out more.

The Brontë Sisters

The Brontë sisters were three English poets and writers. They lived in the 19th century and their books are still famous today. Emily, Charlotte and Anne were born in Thornton, a small village in Yorkshire. The three sisters began writing stories from an early age and they published a book of poems together in 1846, but it wasn't very successful. The first sister to have any success was Charlotte, with her novel *Jane Eyre* (1847). Later that same year, Emily published her one and only novel, *Wuthering Heights* and Anne wrote the book *The Tenant of Wildfell Hall* in 1848. All three sisters died young, Charlotte at the age of 38. The Brontë sisters weren't famous in their lifetimes, but now their books are classic English literature, and people all over the world read them.

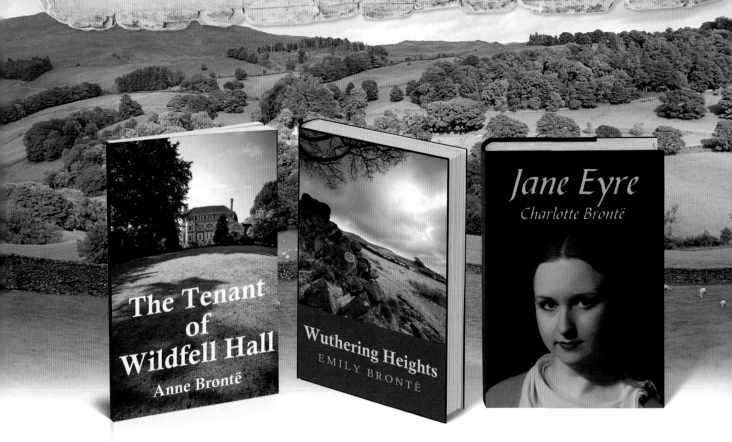

B. Read again and answer the questions.

1. Where was Anne Brontë born?
2. When did the Brontë sisters publish their first book?
3. What kind of book was it?
4. What did Charlotte publish in 1847?
5. Was it successful?
6. How many novels did Emily Brontë write?
7. Which sister wrote a book in 1848?
8. How old was Charlotte Brontë when she died?

C. Find the following words in the text and try to guess what they mean. Then look them up in a dictionary and check your answers. Are they nouns, verbs or adjectives?

poet   village   publish   successful
novel   die   classic

> **TIP**
> Look up unknown words in a dictionary. There, you can find a lot of useful information about a word: pronunciation, word class (noun, verb, etc.), meaning and example sentences.

2 Vocabulary

**Read the note and complete the table.
Can you think of any more words to add?**

> We form many nouns that refer to people
> by adding the suffix -er or -or to a verb.

	Verb	Noun (person)
	write	
		painter
	sing	
	act	
		director
	dance	
		inventor
		explorer

3 Grammar The Past Simple of the verb *to be* → p. 115

A. Read the examples. How do we form the negative and questions?

- **A:** Where **was** Copernicus from? I know he **wasn't** German.
- **B:** He **was** from Poland.
- **A:** **Were** you and Kyle at the museum yesterday?
- **B:** No, we **weren't**. We were at the library.
- There **were** lots of laptops in that store, but there **weren't** any tablets.

B. Complete with *was, wasn't, were* or *weren't*.

1. **A:** Where _____ you yesterday morning?
   B: I _____ at the mall.
   A: _____ you with Lizzie?
   B: No, I _____.

2. **A:** _____ there many people at the beach yesterday?
   B: No, there _____.
   A: _____ it nice?
   B: Yes, it _____. We had a great time. The water _____ really warm.
   A: _____ there a lot of traffic on the road to the beach?
   B: No, there _____. It took only thirty minutes to get there.
   A: That's good.

A. Listen to a radio show about a famous person and answer the questions. Choose a or b. 🔊

1. What did he do?
   a. He was a writer.   **b.** He was a painter.

2. Where was he from?
   a. France   **b.** Spain

3. When was he born?
   a. in 1882   **b.** in 1897

4. When did he die?
   a. in 1913   **b.** in 1963

B. Guessing game

Play in groups of three.

Student A: Choose one of the people in the pictures below, but don't tell Students B and C. Go to page 110 for information about him. Give Students B and C information about this person, and after each statement, they have to try to guess who you are talking about.

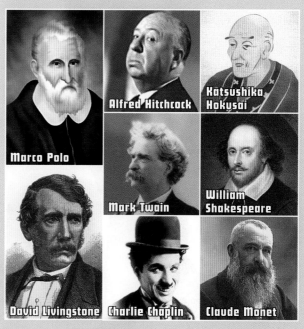

Marco Polo — Alfred Hitchcock — Katsushika Hokusai — Mark Twain — William Shakespeare — David Livingstone — Charlie Chaplin — Claude Monet

Students B and C: Listen to the information Student A tells you about one of the people above and try to guess who that person is.

C. Work in groups. Discuss and write a short biography about a famous person in history. Use some of the prompts below.

- When / born?
- Where / from?
- Where / live?
- What / do?
- What / write, paint, explore, direct, etc.?
- When / die?

D. Present your biography to the rest of the class. Ask other students if they can add any information about that person.

1 Vocabulary 🔊

Match the words with the parts of the body. Then listen and check your answers.

head ☐
arm ☐
leg ☐
hand ☐
foot ☐
mouth ☐
eye ☐
ear ☐
nose ☐
teeth ☐
finger ☐
knee ☐

foot – feet
tooth - teeth

2 Listening 🔊

A. Look at the pictures below. They all have to do with an accident. Guess what happened by checking the sentences that you think are true.

1. The cat jumped out onto the street. ☐
2. The car hit the cat. ☐
3. The motorcycle hit the cat. ☐
4. The car and the motorcycle crashed. ☐
5. The car crashed into the bus stop. ☐
6. The motorcycle crashed into the bus stop. ☐
7. The man fell off the motorcycle. ☐

B. Listen to two friends talking about the accident and check your answers.

C. Listen again and circle the correct options.
1. Tony hurt his **head / hand**.
2. Tony was in his **dad's / brother's** car.
3. The two boys **saw / didn't see** the cat.
4. **A man at the bus stop / The man on the motorcycle** took Tony to the hospital.

3 Speaking

Talk in pairs.

Student A: Imagine you recently had an accident. Tell Student B what happened to you.

Student B: Listen to what happened to Student A and respond using the phrases in the box.

Oh no! That's terrible!
How awful/unlucky!

Really?
I'm sorry to hear that.
Poor you!
Are you OK now?

66 *What's wrong?*
   I had an accident.
Poor you! When did it happen?
   ...
Really? What happened?
   ...
Did you break/hurt anything?
   ...
Did you go...?
   ...
Who...?
   ... 99

TIP

When talking to another person, listen carefully and respond to what he/she is saying (e.g. *Oh no!, That's terrible!*). Also, ask questions to show that you care (e.g. *What happened then?, Did you go to the hospital?*).

4 Writing A paragraph about a bad day

A. Read the paragraph and answer the questions.

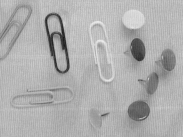

Phil's blog

◀ previous   next ▶

I was very happy when I woke up yesterday. It was my day off, but things went really wrong. First, I decided to make breakfast, but I cut my finger. Luckily, it wasn't serious. Then I rode my bike downtown. I wanted to buy a ticket for last night's baseball game, but the ticket office was closed. After that, I decided to go cycling around the city. However, a car almost hit me on Park Avenue and I fell off my bike. I hurt my knee and hit my head on the sidewalk. Luckily, I didn't break anything. In the end, I went home feeling very sad. It just wasn't my day.

1. How did Phil feel yesterday morning?
2. What happened to him during breakfast?
3. Why didn't he buy a ticket for the baseball game?
4. What did he do after that?
5. What happened when he was on Park Avenue?
6. Did he hurt anything?
7. What did he do in the end?
8. How did he feel?

B. Read the note and complete the paragraph with linking words.

Linking words/phrases
Describe events in the order they happened.
Use linking words/phrases like:
First → After that, Then, Later → In the end

Last Saturday, I visited a small village near Blue Bay beach with some friends. 1 _____, we decided to walk around the village to see it, but Tina fell and hurt her foot. Luckily, it wasn't serious. 2 _____, we wanted to go swimming, but it started raining, so we went to a coffee shop. 3 _____, we went to a restaurant for lunch. However, there was something wrong with the food and I got sick. 4 _____, we went home early. What a day!

C. Think about a bad day, when things went wrong. Use the questions below and keep some notes.

A BAD DAY

First:	
Then:	
Later:	
In the end:	

- Where were you?
- Who were you with?
- What happened?
- What did you do?
- How did you feel?

D. Write a paragraph about a bad day. Use your notes from activity C.

If you don't remember or don't know how to form the Past tense of a verb, check the irregular verbs list on page 117 or look it up in a dictionary.

TIP

Vocabulary

A. Circle the correct words.

1. I only have one can of soda. Do you want to **choose / share** it with me?

2. My cousin studied **Biology / IT**. Maybe he can help you with your laptop.

3. My dad **publishes / teaches** History at a high school.

4. She hurt her **knee / arm** and now she can't walk well.

5. It was a great vacation. I **enjoyed / explored** it.

6. The **inventor / director** made his first movie in 1978.

7. My **tooth / leg** hurts. I think I need to see a dentist.

8. William Cobham is an excellent writer with many **horrible / successful** novels.

Grammar

B. Write the Past Simple of the verbs.

1. invent → _____

2. see → _____

3. die → _____

4. meet → _____

5. begin → _____

6. wear → _____

C. Complete with the Past Simple of the words in parentheses.

A: Where 1 _____ (you, be) yesterday afternoon?
I 2 _____ (try) to call you but you
3 _____ (not answer).

B: Sorry, I 4 _____ (be) at the mall.

A: 5 _____ (you, forget) to take your cell with you?

B: No, I didn't. My sister 6 _____ (take) it with her yesterday morning and she 7 _____ (break) it.

A: How 8 _____ (she, break) it?

B: Don't ask. She 9 _____ (be) on her bike and it
10 _____ (fall) out of her purse.

D. Circle the correct words.

1. Wayne didn't **go / went** to the museum because he was sick.

2. We had an accident on Roseheath Avenue **last / ago** Wednesday.

3. Did you **write / wrote** this poem? It's beautiful!

4. Lily graduated from high school three years **last / ago**.

5. Where did you **find / found** my tablet?

6. **Did / Was** Diane at school yesterday?

Communication

E. Put the dialogue in order.

☐ Because my daughter broke her leg and I want to stay with her.

☐ That's good. How did it happen?

☐ I'm sorry, I can't.

☐ 1 Hey Sam, do you want to go to the movies later?

☐ What's wrong? Why can't you come?

☐ She fell from a tree in our yard.

☐ I'm sorry to hear that. Is she in the hospital?

☐ No, she's at home.

F. Complete the dialogues. Choose a or b.

1. **A:** I saw an old friend from school at the supermarket.
   B: ____
   a. It's a small world.   b. How unlucky!

2. **A:** I cut my finger!
   B: ____
   a. What a day!   b. How awful!

3. **A:** Why are you at home today?
   B: ____
   a. By the way, it's my day off.   b. Because it's my day off.

4. **A:** ____
   B: Really? I'm sorry. I don't think I know you.
   a. You look familiar.   b. What a surprise!

G. Complete the questions for the answers.

1. **A:** _____ that cell phone?
   B: Because it was very cheap.

2. **A:** _____ History?
   B: No, I didn't. I majored in Geography.

3. **A:** _____ lots of new books at the bookstore?
   B: Yes, there were.

4. **A:** _____ your foot?
   B: I hurt it last week.

Self-assessment

Read the following and check the appropriate boxes. For the points you are unsure of, refer back to the relevant sections in the module.

NOW I CAN...

‣ talk about past events/experiences	☐
‣ give reason	☐
‣ talk about famous people in history and their achievements	☐
‣ use suffixes to form nouns that refer to people	☐
‣ write a short biography	☐
‣ talk about accidents	☐
‣ respond to bad news	☐
‣ use linking words/phrases when listing events in order	☐
‣ write about a bad day	☐

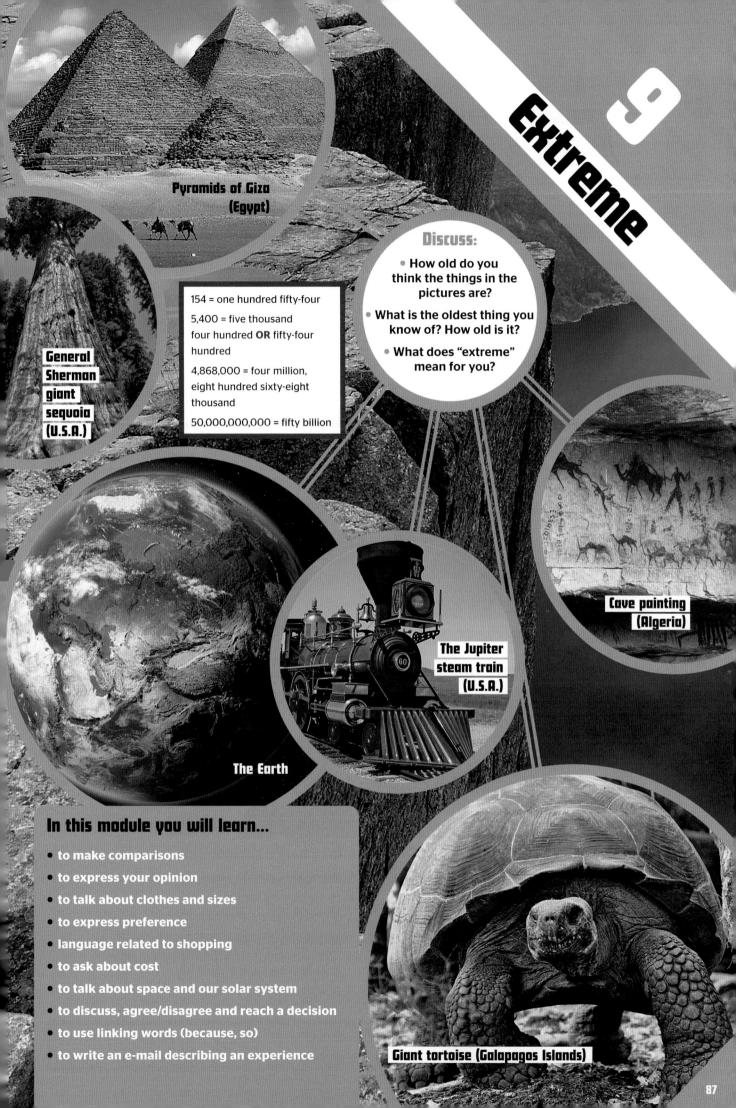

Pyramids of Giza
(Egypt)

General
Sherman
giant
sequoia
(U.S.A.)

154 = one hundred fifty-four

5,400 = five thousand
four hundred **OR** fifty-four
hundred

4,868,000 = four million,
eight hundred sixty-eight
thousand

50,000,000,000 = fifty billion

Discuss:

- How old do you think the things in the pictures are?
- What is the oldest thing you know of? How old is it?
- What does "extreme" mean for you?

Cave painting
(Algeria)

The Jupiter
steam train
(U.S.A.)

The Earth

In this module you will learn...

- to make comparisons
- to express your opinion
- to talk about clothes and sizes
- to express preference
- language related to shopping
- to ask about cost
- to talk about space and our solar system
- to discuss, agree/disagree and reach a decision
- to use linking words (because, so)
- to write an e-mail describing an experience

Giant tortoise (Galapagos Islands)

1 Reading 🔊
A. Listen and read. Who are the shorts for?

BIG SHORTS

Excuse me, do you have men's basketball shorts?

Of course, follow me.

What do you think of these? We have black shorts and red shorts.

How much are they?

The black shorts are $15.99 and the red shorts are more expensive. They're $27.99.

The black shorts are nicer and cheaper than the red shorts. I'll take them.

Great. What size would you like?

These look fine.

Huh? Are you sure?

Maybe not. What size are they?

They're extra large. You need a smaller size than that.

No, no. I'd like extra extra large, please.

Huh?

B. Read again and answer the questions.

1. What kind of shorts does Charlie want?
2. How much are the red shorts?
3. Which shorts are cheaper?
4. Why does Charlie choose the black shorts?
5. What size shorts does the salesperson show Charlie in the beginning?
6. What size shorts does Charlie buy?

Hey, bro! I found some black shorts for you. Really cheap.

Thanks, Charlie.

XS	S	M	L	XL	XXL
extra small - small - medium - large - extra large – extra extra large

2 Vocabulary & Speaking 🔊

A. Listen and discuss the questions.

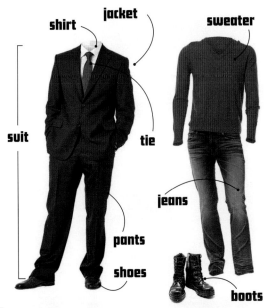

shirt
jacket
sweater
suit
tie
jeans
pants
shoes
boots

baseball cap
dress
T-shirt
skirt
shorts
sneakers

- Which of these clothes do you think are casual and which formal?
- Which of these clothes do you usually wear? Which do you never wear?

> The words **pants**, **shorts** and **jeans** are plural nouns.

B. Listen. Then say how much you usually pay for some of the clothes above.

$7.99	=	seven dollars and ninety-nine cents (seven ninety-nine)
€45.75	=	forty-five euros and seventy-five cents (forty-five seventy-five)
£90.55	=	ninety pounds and fifty-five pence (ninety fifty-five)

3 Grammar Comparative forms → p. 116

A. Look at the pictures and complete the sentences with the words *red* or *green*. What word comes after the comparative form of adjectives?

$50

$35

> The _____ T-shirt is **bigger than** the _____ T-shirt.
>
> The _____ T-shirt is **more expensive than** the _____ T-shirt.

B. Complete the table with the correct form of the adjectives.

Adjective	Comparative Form
tall	taller
old	_____
large	larger
nice	_____
slim	slimmer
hot	_____
dirty	dirtier
happy	_____
beautiful	more beautiful
careful	_____
good	better
bad	worse
far	farther/further

C. Complete with the comparative form of the adjectives in parentheses.

1. **A:** I think the black shoes are _____ (modern) than the blue shoes.

   B: Yeah, but the blue shoes are _____ (cheap).

2. **A:** Is your new house _____ (big) than your old house?

   B: Yes, it is. It has lots of rooms but the backyard is _____ (small).

3. **A:** It's _____ (sunny) today than it was yesterday.

   B: Yes, but it's _____ (cold).

4. **A:** Your sister is very good at ping-pong. Are you good at ping-pong, too?

   B: No. Stacey's _____ (good) than me.

> Ted is taller than me. = Ted is taller than I am.

4 Speaking Role play

Talk in groups of three.

Students A and B go to page 107.

Student C go to page 109.

1 Vocabulary 🔊

Can you name the planets in our Solar System? Listen and check your answers.

Jupiter   Neptune   Venus   Mercury   Saturn   Mars   Uranus

sun

galaxy

Moon

star

Earth

2 Reading 🔊

A. Do the quiz and test your knowledge. Then listen and check your answers.

COSMIC QUIZ!

Our solar system has eight planets: Mercury, Venus, Earth, Mars, Jupiter, Saturn, Uranus and Neptune. One of the most important discoveries in astronomy and science was that the planets move around the sun. But who discovered this?

a Galileo Galilei

b Nicolaus Copernicus

c Johannes Kepler

Jupiter is the largest planet in our solar system and also the third brightest object in the night sky. You can see Jupiter with the naked eye, without a telescope. How many Earths fit inside Jupiter?

a about one hundred

b over one thousand

c over one million

Neptune is the farthest planet from the Sun and also the coldest. It is a very windy place and temperatures can reach -364°F! The hottest planet in our solar system has temperatures of about 860°F. Which planet is this?

a Mercury

b Venus

c Mars

The planet with the shortest day is Jupiter. A day on Jupiter only lasts 9.9 Earth hours. The planet with the longest day is Venus. A year on Venus is shorter than a year on Earth and lasts 225 Earth days. But how long is one day on Venus?

a 243 Earth minutes

b 243 Earth hours

c 243 Earth days

B. Read again and write T for True or F for False.

1. Jupiter is the largest and brightest planet in our solar system.
2. Neptune has temperatures of about -860°F.
3. It is very windy on Neptune.
4. An Earth day is longer than a day on Jupiter.
5. An Earth year is longer than a year on Venus.

3 Grammar Superlative forms → p. 116

A. Read the examples below. How do we form the superlative form of adjectives?

> Mercury is **the closest** planet to the Sun.
>
> I think Saturn is **the most beautiful** planet in our solar system.

B. Complete the table with the correct form of the adjectives.

Adjective	Comparative Form	Superlative Form
bright	brighter	
		the closest
big		
	easier	
important		the most important
good		the best
	worse	the worst
	farther/further	the farthest/furthest

C. Complete with the correct form of the adjectives in parentheses.

1. The Science Museum is the _____ (popular) museum in the city.

2. The red dress is _____ (modern) than the blue dress, but your black dress is the _____ (modern) of the three.

3. Tonight the stars in the sky are _____ (bright) than any other night.

4. Saturn has 62 moons. Titan is the _____ (large) moon. It is _____ (large) than Mercury.

5. Go to Danny's Coffee Shop for ice cream. It has the _____ (good) ice cream in town.

4 Listening & Speaking ◀))

A. Look at the information in the table below. Then listen to a teacher talking to his class. Which planet is the teacher talking about?

	AVERAGE TEMPERATURE (°F)	SIZE-DIAMETER (miles)	DISTANCE FROM SUN (miles)
MERCURY	333	3,032	36,000,000
VENUS	867	7,521	67,000,000
EARTH	59	7,926	93,000,000
MARS	-85	4,221	142,000,000
JUPITER	-166	88,846	484,000,000
SATURN	-220	74,897	891,000,000
URANUS	-320	31,763	1,785,000,000
NEPTUNE	-330	30,775	2,793,000,000

B. GUESSING GAME Talk in pairs.

Student A: Choose four planets from the table above, but don't tell Student B. Then describe the planets to Student B, as in the example. You have two minutes. How many planets did he/she guess correctly?

Student B: Listen to Student A's descriptions and try to guess the planets. How many planets did you guess correctly in two minutes?

> 66 *It's bigger than Neptune, but it isn't the biggest planet in our solar system.*
> ***Is it Saturn?***
> *Wrong! It's one of the coldest planets.*
> ***I know! It's Uranus.***
> *Correct! Next one. It's...* 99

TIP
Before you speak, make sure you understand the task and how you should use the prompts.

91

1 Reading 🔊

A. Read the website quickly and match the headings a-d with the paragraphs 1-4. Then listen and check your answers.

a. What are they like?
b. Why are they endangered?
c. Where do they live?
d. What can we do to help?

TIP
Read the text quickly to understand the main idea.

Help Save Snow Leopards!

Name:	Snow Leopard
Location:	Central Asia
Population:	4,000-6,500 in the wild
Status:	endangered

These big cats live in one of the most extreme places in the world. They live high in the mountains between 8,000 and 22,000 feet. Their long, thick fur protects them from the extreme cold and keeps them warm. Their extra large paws help them walk on the snow, like snowshoes.

Snow leopards are shy, lonely animals and they are very difficult to find and take a picture of in the wild. They eat wild sheep and goats and are very good hunters. They can run fast, climb, jump 30 to 50 feet or even walk 27 miles in one night to find food!

There are lots of reasons. Firstly, hunters kill these beautiful cats for their fur. Also, it is often difficult for snow leopards to find food because people destroy their habitat. So, when snow leopards can't find animals in the wild, they kill farm animals. And as a result, farmers kill them.

TIP
Read the text carefully to understand specific details.

There are different things you can do:
- Join an organization. They try to help both the local people and protect snow leopards.
- Become a volunteer and help at different events.
- Donate money to an organization.
- Buy things from an organization.
- Adopt a snow leopard.
- Tell others about this endangered species. That helps, too!

B. Read again and answer the questions about snow leopards.

1. How does their fur help them?
2. Why can't we take pictures of them in the wild easily?
3. What do they eat?
4. How far can they jump?
5. What do they do when they can't find food in the wild?
6. Why do farmers kill them?
7. What do volunteers do?

2 Vocabulary 🔊

Listen. Do any of these animals live in your country?

deer - deer (plural)
sheep - sheep (plural)

3 Pronunciation 🔊

A. Listen and repeat. Notice the difference in pronunciation.

/ɪ/	live
/iː/	leave

B. Say the words below. In which category do they belong? Listen and check your answers.

sh**ee**p   g**o**rilla   p**i**cture   p**eo**ple

f**ee**t   k**i**ll   d**o**lphin   k**ee**p   r**ea**ch

A. Listen to a brother and a sister talking about mountain gorillas and complete the sentences. 🔊

TIP
Before you listen, try to predict what kind of information is missing.

1. Mountain gorillas live in central east _____.

2. Hunters kill them for their _____ and _____.

3. There are only _____ mountain gorillas in the wild.

4. At first, Eddie wants to _____.

5. In the end, Eddie and Carol decide to get _____ for their friends.

6. They want to get _____ for Richard.

B. Work in pairs. Imagine that you and your partner want to help an organization that supports mountain gorillas. Below are some of the items they sell on their website. Choose 3 of your classmates, discuss and decide what you want to buy for each of them. Give reasons. Use some of the phrases given below.

stuffed animal $16
book $30
T-shirt $20
baseball cap $15
poster $8
DVD $35

❝ *I think a... is a nice/good present for Tony.*
The best thing to buy him is a... because he likes/reads...
Let's buy/get him a... . It's nicer / better / more useful.
I think he needs a... so how about getting him a...?
That looks like a nice/useful/interesting present.
What do you think? ❞

❝ *I agree. / Nice idea. / You're right.*
I don't agree. / I don't think so.
Yes, but Tony hates...
I have a better idea. We can get him a... because... ❞

C. Tell the class what you decided to buy for three of your classmates and why.

❝ *We decided to get a... for... because...* ❞

1 Vocabulary & Speaking 🔊

A. Listen. Which of these sports do you think are extreme?

mountain biking

hang gliding

skydiving

rock climbing

sailing

surfing

scuba diving

B. Talk in small groups. What do you think about the sports above? Discuss using some of the adjectives in the box.

exciting	difficult
boring	easy
dangerous	popular
safe	

❝ *I really like... It's very exciting.*
No way! ... is more exciting.
I agree but it's also more dangerous than... ❞

2 Listening 🔊

A. Listen to a dialogue between a man and a woman at a rock climbing school. Match to make two true sentences.

	is a rock climbing instructor.
The man	is the school secretary.
The woman	wants to learn rock climbing.
	is a student.

TIP
While listening, try to understand the general idea, not every single word.

B. Listen again and circle the correct words.

1. The rock climbing school doesn't have an **inside / outside** climbing wall.

2. The man **knows / doesn't know** a lot about rock climbing.

3. The man thinks rock climbing is **safe / dangerous**.

4. The man wants to start **tomorrow / next week**.

5. Sam is **a student / an instructor** at the school.

6. The man **wants / doesn't want** to meet Sam.

3 Writing An e-mail describing an experience

A. Read the e-mail below and complete the paragraph.

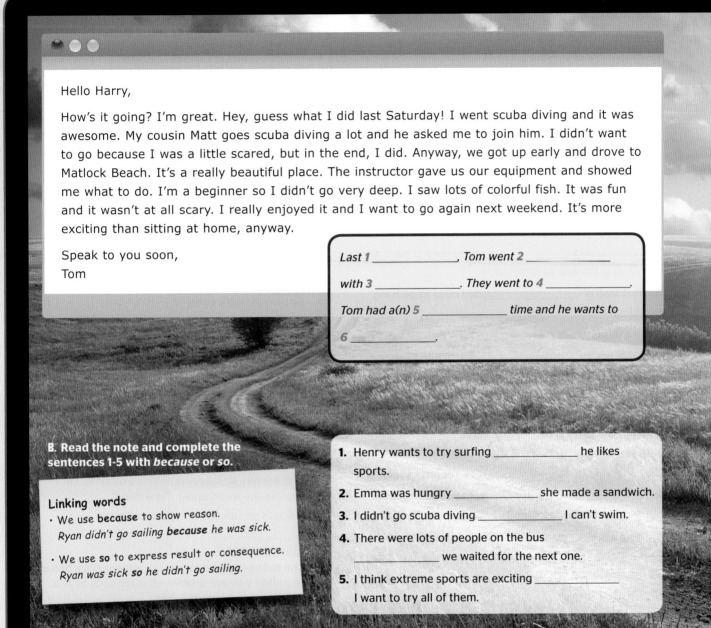

Hello Harry,

How's it going? I'm great. Hey, guess what I did last Saturday! I went scuba diving and it was awesome. My cousin Matt goes scuba diving a lot and he asked me to join him. I didn't want to go because I was a little scared, but in the end, I did. Anyway, we got up early and drove to Matlock Beach. It's a really beautiful place. The instructor gave us our equipment and showed me what to do. I'm a beginner so I didn't go very deep. I saw lots of colorful fish. It was fun and it wasn't at all scary. I really enjoyed it and I want to go again next weekend. It's more exciting than sitting at home, anyway.

Speak to you soon,
Tom

Last 1 _____, Tom went 2 _____ with 3 _____. They went to 4 _____.

Tom had a(n) 5 _____ time and he wants to

6 _____.

B. Read the note and complete the sentences 1-5 with *because* or *so*.

Linking words
- We use **because** to show reason.
  Ryan didn't go sailing **because** he was sick.

- We use **so** to express result or consequence.
  Ryan was sick **so** he didn't go sailing.

1. Henry wants to try surfing _____ he likes sports.
2. Emma was hungry _____ she made a sandwich.
3. I didn't go scuba diving _____ I can't swim.
4. There were lots of people on the bus _____ we waited for the next one.
5. I think extreme sports are exciting _____ I want to try all of them.

C. Talk in pairs. Think of an interesting activity you tried in the past and discuss the questions below.

- What activity did you try?
- When did you go?
- Where did you go?
- Who did you go with?
- What was it like?
- Do you want to try it again?

D. Write an e-mail to a friend describing a past experience. Use your ideas from activity C.

Vocabulary

A. Cross out the odd word. Then add one more.

1. sweater – skirt – shorts – formal - _____
2. farmer – deer – sheep – camel - _____
3. telescope – star – moon – planet - _____
4. pence – cent – million – euro - _____
5. sailing – surfing – exciting – skydiving - _____

B. Complete with the words in the box.

equipment donated colorful lonely
temperature discovered

1. Who _____ Neptune?
2. My parents _____ $1,000 to help save the Giant panda.
3. Richard is very _____. He doesn't have any friends in his new neighborhood.
4. What kind of _____ do I need to go hang gliding?
5. I like this dress. It's very _____.
6. Yesterday the _____ reached 104°F. It was very hot!

C. Circle the correct words.

1. Animals die because people **destroy / adopt** their habitats.
2. I don't want to watch that movie. It's **scared / scary**.
3. There's the sailing **hunter / instructor**. Ask him about taking some lessons.
4. There are eight planets in our **solar / sun** system.
5. These jeans don't **fit / follow** me. I need a bigger size.

Grammar

D. Complete with the correct form of the adjectives in parentheses.

1. Saturday is the _____ (busy) day of the week at the store.
2. The book is _____ (interesting) than the movie.
3. Mount Everest is the _____ (high) mountain in the world.
4. Jack Miller has the _____ (modern) car in my neighborhood.
5. Are you _____ (young) or _____ (old) than your sister?

E. Circle the correct words.

1. Mountain biking is easier **from / than** rock climbing.
2. This is the **more / most** expensive T-shirt in the store.
3. Mark is **the / the most** tallest of all my friends.
4. I'll take the blue shirt. It's **cheaper / more cheaper**.

Communication

F. Complete the dialogues with the phrases in the box.

a. No way!
b. What size is it?
c. How much is it?
d. Come on, what do you think?
e. Do you need a bigger size?
f. I don't agree.
g. What do you think of these?
h. I'll take it.

1. **A:** Excuse me. I'm looking for a casual shirt. Do you have any?
   B: Of course, follow me. **1** _____
   A: They're nice. I like this pink shirt. **2** _____
   B: Extra small. **3** _____
   A: No, it's OK. It's not for me. It's for my sister. She wears extra small.
   B: OK, then.
   A: **4** _____
   B: Well, it's not very expensive, only $30.
   A: **5** _____

2. **A:** This vacation is boring. Let's go scuba diving.
   B: What? **6** _____ It's dangerous. Let's go mountain biking. It's safer.
   A: **7** _____ Mountain biking can be pretty dangerous and anyway scuba diving is more exciting. Let's explore the world under the water. **8** _____
   B: OK, let's go talk to the instructor first.

Self-assessment
Read the following and check the appropriate boxes. For the points you are unsure of, refer back to the relevant sections in the module.

NOW I CAN...	
make comparisons	☐
express my opinion	☐
talk about clothes and sizes	☐
express preference	☐
use language related to shopping	☐
ask about cost	☐
talk about space and our solar system	☐
discuss, agree/disagree and reach a decision	☐
use linking words (because, so)	☐
write an e-mail describing an experience	☐

10

Get away

camping

skiing

backpacking

sightseeing tour

by a beach

cruise

97

Discuss:

- What kind of vacation did you go on last year?
- What is your favorite kind of vacation?
- What do you usually do?

In this module you will learn...

- to talk about dates and seasons
- to say your date of birth
- to locate information on tickets, schedules, etc.
- to talk and write about your future plans and arrangements
- to invite someone to do something
- to accept or refuse invitations
- to ask for and give advice
- to prioritize and express your opinion
- to talk and write about your vacations

1 Vocabulary 🔊

A. Listen. Which season is best for going on vacation?

winter

spring

summer

fall

B. Listen. Which months make up the four seasons in your country?

January	May	September
February	June	October
March	July	November
April	August	December

2 Speaking

Talk in pairs.

> *What's the date today/tomorrow?*
> **It's April 30th.**
> *When were you born?*
> **I was born on May 22nd, 1994.**

Dates: We write: *April 30th*
We say: *April 30th* or *the 30th of April*
in + seasons/months/years
on + dates

---

3 Reading

A. Look at the things on Jay's desk. Where is Jay going? Who is he going with?

Your booking confirmation

Reservation information

Book date: **Friday, May 17**
Confirmation number: KLY331
Status: CONFIRMED

Flight details

Departing Flight

Philadelphia Toronto
2:45p.m.   3:35p.m.
Friday, May 24
Flight number: **VY7564**

Return Flight
Toronto   Philadelphia

Air Canada Center
•Hockey Fina
Toronto Maple Le
vs.
Boston Bruin

Air Canada Center
•Hockey Final•
Toronto Maple Leafs
vs.
Boston Bruins

May
25th
PUCK DROP 7P.M.

Row G
Seat 88

Row G
Seat 87 $45.00

Friday May 24th

8 a.m.
9
10
11
12 p.m.
1
2
3
4
5
6
7
8
9
10
11

Visit CN Tower

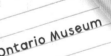

Saturday May 25th

8 a.m.
9
10
11
12 p.m.
1
2
3
4
5
6
7
8
9

Royal Ontario Museum

Lunch with cousin Tom

GO LEAFS GO!

MAP OF TORONTO

From: Jay
To: Carl

Flight time: 2:45
Meet at airport at 1:30?
Don't forget your camera!

Sent 9:02a.m.

B. Look at the things again and write T for True or F for False.

> Make sure you read all the information given carefully. When doing the activity, decide where you can find the information/details you need.
>
> **TIP**

1. Jay and Carl are going to take an airplane to Toronto on Friday. ☐
2. They are going to arrive there at 2:45 on Friday afternoon. ☐
3. Jay is going to stay at a friend's house. ☐
4. Jay is going to visit a museum on Saturday morning. ☐
5. Jay and Carl are going to watch a hockey game on Friday evening. ☐
6. The Toronto Maple Leafs are going to play the Boston Bruins. ☐
7. Jay is going to visit the CN Tower on May 24th. ☐

4 Grammar Future *going to* (affirmative - negative) → *p. 116*

A. Read the examples. How do we form the affirmative and negative of the Future *going to*?

> Harriet **is going to travel** to Brazil in the summer, but she **isn't going to stay** in Rio.
>
> John and Lee **are going to watch** a soccer game tonight. They **aren't going to watch** a DVD.

> It isn't necessary to say or write **to go** with the Future *going to*.
> *I'm going (to go) to London next Saturday.*

B. Complete with the Future *going to* of the verbs in parentheses.

1. Amy _____ (not arrive) in Madrid on Sunday.
   She _____ (get) there on Monday morning.

2. **A:** Are these airplane tickets?
   B: Yes, Roger and I _____ (visit) Paris in the spring.

3. **A:** Do you want to get a pizza after work?
   B: No, thanks. I _____ (go) to my sister's house.
   She _____ (cook) chicken for dinner.

4. **A:** Do you want me to give you a ride to the train station?
   B: Thanks, but I _____ (not take) the train.
   I _____ (drive) there.

5. **A:** Diane and I _____ (buy) tickets for the Winter Olympics in February.
   B: Really? I _____ (watch) them on TV.

5 Pronunciation ◀))
A. Listen and repeat. Notice the difference in pronunciation.

/θ/	mon**th**
/ð/	wea**th**er

B. Say the words below. In which category do they belong? Listen and check your answers.

these   **thousand**   Ear**th**   mo**th**er   clo**th**es

third   heal**th**y   toge**th**er   ba**th**room   bo**th**

6 Speaking & Writing
A. Talk in pairs. Make plans for a two-day trip. Decide:
- where to go
- when to go (season, exact date)
- how to travel

66 *Let's go to... and travel around.*
     No, I went there two years ago. How about going to...?
Nice idea! Let's go in the spring. The weather is beautiful then. **99**

B. Tell the class about your plans.
66 *We're going to travel to... We're going to take the...* **99**

C. Write a short e-mail to a friend telling him/her about your plans.

1 Vocabulary 🔊

A. Listen. Can you think of any examples of these geographical features?

mountain

island   **ocean/sea**

lake   **forest**   **river**   **town**

B. Listen. Decide where you can do these activities. Use vocabulary from above. Which of the following do you do when you go on vacation?

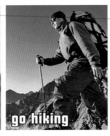

buy souvenirs/postcards | go sightseeing | go hiking | go fishing | do water sports | taste local food

2 Reading 🔊

A. Listen and read. Where is each dialogue taking place? Match.

| **a.** at a castle | **b.** on a street with stores | **c.** at a hotel |

 1

Tom Hey Steve, are you going to go hiking in the forest?
Steve Yes, I am, but later in the afternoon. I'm going to have lunch first. Would you like to join me?
Tom Of course! Where are we going to eat?
Steve At that place on the corner with local food.
Tom Nice. Wait here, I'm just going to get my wallet from my room, OK?
Steve OK, see you in a while.

 2

Kim So, what else?
Sue I'd like to get something for my sister. Are you going to buy anything else?
Kim Maybe. I really like those T-shirts over there. I'm going to get one. Do you want to come?
Sue Sure, why not? I can see some nice souvenirs. Maybe I can find something for my sister.

 3

Nina So, did you like it or did you get bored?
Lucy It was all right, but the ticket was kind of expensive, don't you think?
Nina Yes, but the furniture and the rooms were beautiful.
Lucy What are we going to do next? No more sightseeing. I'm tired.
Nina Stop complaining! There are lots of things to see in this city. So, which museum are we going to visit now? Would you like to visit the National Museum or the Museum of Modern Art?
Lucy Sorry, maybe tomorrow. I have other plans. I'm going to go for coffee.

> **TIP**
> Find key words in the dialogues. They help you to understand the main ideas.

B. Read again and answer the questions.

1. What is Steve going to do today?
2. Does Tom accept Steve's invitation?
3. What are Tom and Steve going to have for lunch?
4. Where is Tom's wallet?
5. Why does Kim want to go to the store?
6. Why does Sue go with her?
7. What did Lucy think of the castle?
8. What does Nina want to do now?
9. Why doesn't Lucy want to go with her?

> We use *Do you want to...?* and *Would you like to...?* to make invitations.

3 Grammar Future *going to* (questions) → *p. 116*

A. Read the examples. How do we form short answers?

> **A:** What **are you going to buy** from the souvenir store?
> **B:** I'm not sure.
>
> **Are you going to swim** in the river? 〈 Yes, I am.
>   No, I'm not.

B. Complete the dialogues with the Future *going to* of the verbs in parentheses. Give short answers where possible.

1. **A:** _____ you _____ (send) any postcards to your friends back home?

   B: No, _____. I send them e-mails almost every day.

2. **A:** What _____ you _____ (do) this afternoon?

   B: I don't know.

   A: My brother _____ (go) fishing and I'm thinking of going with him. Would you like to come?

   B: OK. _____ he _____ (drive) to Hunnington Lake?

   A: Yes, _____. Don't worry. He _____ (give) us a ride there and back.

3. **A:** _____ Mary _____ (go) hiking this weekend?

   B: No, _____. She _____ (stay) home. She's very tired these days.

4 Listening 🔊

A. Listen to a conversation between a husband and wife. Check the activities they decide to do tomorrow.

go sightseeing ☐
go swimming ☐
do water sports ☐
buy souvenirs ☐
taste local food ☐
go fishing ☐

> **TIP**
> Don't assume that an answer is correct just because the speakers mention a word/phrase that is in the activity. Listen carefully before you answer.

B. Listen again and complete the sentences.

1. The man and woman are staying at a _____.

2. _____ is the last day of their vacation.

3. In the morning, they are going to _____ and in the afternoon they are going to _____.

4. *Ronaldo's* is a great place to have _____.

5. The man is going to go _____ at night.

5 Speaking

Talk in groups of three. Use phrases from the boxes.

Student A: Invite Students B and C to do something together. Use ideas from activity 1B or your own and discuss them.

Student B: Accept Student A's invitation and discuss his/her plans.

Student C: Refuse Student A's invitation and tell him/her about your own plans.

> 66 *Would you like to... with me tomorrow?*
>
>   *Yes, I'd love to. What time/Where/What/How are we going to...?*
>
> *... What about you? Do you want to...?*
>
>   *I'm sorry, I can't. I'm going to...*
>
> *Really? Are you going to...?* 99

Inviting	Accepting an invitation	Refusing an invitation
Would you like to...?	Yes, I'd love to.	I'm sorry, I can't.
Do you want to...?	Sure, why not?	I'm afraid I'm busy/tired.
	Of course!	Sorry, I have other plans.
	Sounds awesome/great!	No, thanks.
	Great idea!	Maybe some other time.
	Thanks for inviting me.	Isn't it kind of boring/dangerous?

1 Vocabulary 🔊

Listen. Which of the following are important to have with you when traveling to another country? Can you think of anything else to add?

passport

map

sunscreen

phrasebook

first-aid kit

credit card

flashlight

suitcase

swimsuit

2 Reading 🔊

A. Read and match the problems 1-3 with the advice a-c. Then listen and check your answers.

Advice for travelers going abroad

1 ☐
Next week I'm going skiing in Canada. It's my first time. What should I take with me?

Jack, Houston

2 ☐
I'm going to Peru next summer. I'm going to stay with a local family and teach in a school. I don't know very much about Peru or traveling abroad. Any advice?

Hank, Orlando

3 ☐
I am going on a trip to Hawaii with my husband. The flight to the island is 9 hours long and I'm kind of worried. What should we do to make the long flight relaxing?

Rose, Miami

a
Make sure you drink lots of water, and every hour you should get up and walk around. Take a good book with you and some relaxing music to listen to. You can also try to sleep and wake up when you arrive!

b
First of all, it's going to be cold so take warm clothes. Also, be careful! The sun is very strong up in the mountains, so you should take lots of sunscreen. You shouldn't worry about equipment because you can rent that at the resort.

c
Before you visit a country for the first time, you should learn about the culture and also learn to speak a few words in the language. You should also find out about the necessary travel documents to enter the country, such as a visa, etc.

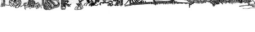

B. Read again and answer the questions.

1. How long is the flight from Miami to Hawaii?
2. What should you do for exercise during a flight?
3. Why should Jack take sunscreen with him?
4. What can you rent at a ski resort?
5. What should you know before traveling to a country abroad?

3 Grammar The verb *should* → *p. 116*

A. Read the examples. What do you notice about the verb that comes after *should*?

A: I'm going to travel to Moscow. What **should I take** with me?

B: You **should take** lots of warm clothes. And you **shouldn't forget** your passport.

B. Complete with *should* or *shouldn't* and the verbs in parentheses.

1. **A:** I want to go to the beach tomorrow.

   B: You _____ (take) some sunscreen with you.

2. **A:** It's lunchtime but I'm not hungry.

   B: You _____ (stop) eating all those snacks.

3. **A:** It's very difficult for me to get up in the morning.

   B: You _____ (watch) TV till late every night.

4. **A:** It's Gloria's graduation on Friday.

   B: We _____ (buy) her a present.

4 Pronunciation 🔊

A. Listen and repeat. Which letters are silent?

a. should   **b.** island

B. Read the words and underline the silent letters. Then listen and check your answers.

listen   flight   know   castle

wrong   science   hour   high

walk   answer

A. Look at the advertisement and discuss the questions.

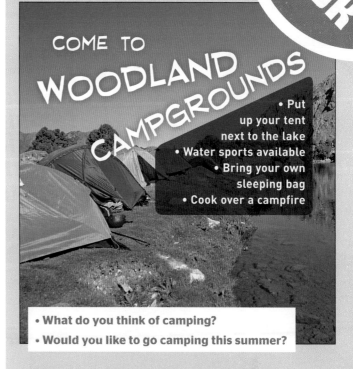

COME TO
WOODLAND
CAMPGROUNDS

• Put up your tent next to the lake
• Water sports available
• Bring your own sleeping bag
• Cook over a campfire

• **What do you think of camping?**
• **Would you like to go camping this summer?**

B. Look at the items below and listen to four people talking about one of the most important things to take with you when going camping. Write the item next to the name. 🔊

MATCHES

first aid

Peter: _____   Jenny: _____

Vicky: _____   Roger: _____

C. Talk in pairs. Imagine you are going on a camping trip. Apart from essential camping equipment, you can only take 5 of the items shown above. Discuss what you should take with you and why with your partner. Use the phrases given.

❝ *I think we should/shouldn't take… because…*
I believe we definitely need… because…
… is/are useful/necessary/important because …
We're going to… so we should take… ❞

D. Report what you are going to take on your camping trip to the class. Give reasons.

1 Speaking

Talk in groups of three. Read the vacation advertisements and the descriptions of the people below. Discuss and decide which vacation is best for each of them. Give reasons.

1 week skiing in the mountains

2-week camping vacation on an island

5 ★ Hotel by the beach for 2 weeks

Monaco · Naples · Barcelona · Athens

3-week cruise around the Mediterranean

> *The best vacation for... is the...*
> *I agree. He/She likes... and...*
> *What about the...?*
> *No, I don't think it's a good idea because... doesn't like...*

a two-week vacation
~~a two-weeks vacation~~

> **Bessie** loves traveling and enjoys warm weather. She isn't very active but she enjoys swimming in a pool. She wants to visit different places, so she needs a long vacation to do this.

> **Wendy** needs a vacation to relax. She wants to eat nice meals and sleep in a comfortable bed. She likes swimming in the ocean but she prefers a pool. She doesn't really enjoy traveling around.

> **Tony** is a History major and is looking for a cheap vacation. He loves hot weather and he wants to stay near the beach. However, he doesn't really like big hotels.

> **Ray** loves spending time in nature and doing extreme sports. He doesn't have a lot of time off work and he doesn't really like hot weather.

2 Listening 🔊

A. Listen to Colin talking to his friend Adrian on the phone about his vacation on the island of Crete. Which of the following does he talk about?

the food ☐
the weather ☐
the people ☐
the hotel ☐
souvenirs ☐
water sports ☐

B. Listen again and choose a or b.

1. Colin spent the first day ____.
   a. at the beach   b. at the hotel swimming pool

2. At the beach, ____ went scuba diving.
   a. Colin   b. Colin's brother

3. Colin is going to ____ today.
   a. do water sports   b. go hiking

4. Colin really likes the ____ in Crete.
   a. fish   b. cheese

5. Colin is going to buy Adrian a ____.
   a. book   b. T-shirt

3 Writing An e-mail while on vacation

A. Read the e-mail and complete the table. Write *yesterday*, *today* or *tomorrow*.

see a whale shark	
play tennis	
have a barbecue on the beach	
visit some islands	
spend the day at the hotel	
go fishing	

To: Mary
Add Cc   Add Bcc
Subject: Maldives!!!!!!!!!!
Attach a file

Hi Mary,

I'm having the perfect vacation here in the Maldives. The weather is amazing and the beaches are fantastic. Yesterday, I went on a fishing trip with Amy. We didn't catch anything, but we saw a whale shark, and it was huge! I took lots of pictures. Then in the evening we had a barbecue on the beach. The sunset was amazing. Today, we're going to stay at the hotel all day and later I'm going to play tennis with Amy. There are some beautiful courts here at the hotel. (I always win! 😊 She hates losing!) Tomorrow, we have a busy day. We're going to go sailing around some of the islands. I'm so excited! We're going to jump off the boat and swim in the clear blue water.

Jealous? Well, next time come with us!

See you when I get home,
Karen

B. Read the note and say which of the words/ phrases in the red box refer to the past and which refer to the future.

Using tenses

When writing, be careful which tenses you use.
• Use the **Past Simple** to describe what you did.
• Use the **Future *going to*** for your future plans.

tomorrow	two days ago	yesterday	soon
in 2011	in two days	last night	next week

Now expand the notes into sentences.

1. Lydia / visit / castle / yesterday morning

   _____

2. last summer / we / stay / hotel / by / river

   _____

3. cousins and I / travel / around Europe / next month

   _____

4. we / go / on / cruise / three weeks ago

   _____

5. the boys / try / hang gliding / tomorrow morning

   _____

C. Talk in pairs. Imagine you are on vacation and your partner calls you. Discuss the questions given. You can keep notes if you like.

• Where are you?
• When did you arrive there?
• How did you get there?
• What did you do yesterday?
• What did you do / are you going to do today?
• What are you going to do tomorrow?
• When are you going to get back?

yesterday	
today	
tomorrow	

D. Imagine you are on vacation. Write an e-mail to a friend telling him/her about it. Use the ideas you discussed in activity C.

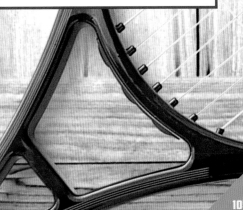

Vocabulary

A. Circle the correct words.

1. Hang gliding is dangerous. Be **careful / comfortable**!

2. We want to **taste / travel** abroad this summer.

3. Give me a **tent / flashlight**. I can't see anything in here.

4. **Make / Get** sure you have your passport with you.

5. Let's go on a tour around the **ocean / island**.

6. You should always take **sunset / sunscreen** with you when you go to the beach.

B. Complete with the words in the box.

| excited   barbecue   catch   souvenirs |
| win   bored |

1. I'm _____. Do you want to go mountain biking?

2. Let's have a _____ in our backyard tonight.

3. I'm very _____. I'm going to Brazil!

4. My dad visits lots of countries and he always brings me _____ .

5. Did your team _____ or lose?

6. John went fishing but didn't _____ any fish!

Grammar

C. Complete with the Future *going to* of the verbs in the box.

| not swim   buy   arrive   stay   come |
| not visit   take |

1. My roommate _____ back from his vacation tonight. He _____ at midnight.

2. We _____ the Science Museum. We don't have time.

3. _____ you _____ a first-aid kit with you on your camping trip?

4. Diane _____ a phrasebook before she goes to Spain because she doesn't speak Spanish.

5. _____ he _____ at a hotel by the beach?

6. Fred _____ in the river. He's scared.

D. Complete the situations. Use *should/shouldn't* and the verbs in the box.

| take   buy   sit   go   call   listen |

1. **A:** I'm very tired today.

   B: Well, you _____ hiking then.

2. **A:** I'm going to go sightseeing tomorrow.

   B: You _____ a map before you go.

3. **A:** I lost my credit card.

   B: Oh, no! You _____ the bank.

4. **A:** My head hurts again.

   B: Well, you _____ in the sun all day.

5. **A:** I can't sleep at night.

   B: You _____ to some relaxing music. It helps.

6. **A:** I want to go rock climbing.

   B: Really? You _____ lessons first.

Communication

E. Choose a or b.

1. **A:** Would you like to go for a walk by the river?

   B: ____ It's a beautiful day.

   a. I'd love to.   **b.** Maybe some other time.

2. **A:** Do you want to go skiing next weekend?

   B: ____ I'm going camping with Ted.

   a. Sorry, I have other plans.   **b.** Sure, why not?

3. **A:** Would you like to watch a hockey game?

   B: ____ I'm afraid I'm busy.

   a. Thanks for inviting me.   **b.** No, thanks.

F. Match.

1. What's the date?	☐
2. Are you going to stay at a hotel?	☐
3. I'm worried.	☐
4. When are you going to leave?	☐
5. I'm going to go skiing. Any advice?	☐
6. How long is your flight?	☐

a. No, I prefer camping.

b. Two hours.

c. You should always listen to the instructor.

d. It's November 20th.

e. You should try to relax.

f. On August 3rd.

Self-assessment

Read the following and check the appropriate boxes. For the points you are unsure of, refer back to the relevant sections in the module.

NOW I CAN...	
‣ talk about dates and seasons	☐
‣ say my date of birth	☐
‣ locate information on tickets, schedules, etc.	☐
‣ talk and write about my future plans and arrangements	☐
‣ invite someone to do something	☐
‣ accept or refuse invitations	☐
‣ ask for and give advice	☐
‣ talk and write about my vacations	☐

1b Pair work Guessing game

Talk in pairs.

Student A: Read the information below and choose which person you want to be. Don't tell Student B.
Student B: Ask questions and guess who Student A is.

NAME: James Burton

JOB: doctor

WORKPLACE: Downsville Hospital

NAME: Anna Richards

JOB: nurse

WORKPLACE: Adbury Hospital

NAME: Kelly Bird
JOB: waitress
WORKPLACE: Al's Restaurant

NAME: Kyle Shipton

JOB: doctor

WORKPLACE: Adbury Hospital

NAME: Olivia Flint

JOB: waitress

WORKPLACE: Lisa's Restaurant

NAME: Gary Skinner
JOB: chef
WORKPLACE: Al's Restaurant

❝ *Are you a nurse?*
  No, I'm not.
Are you a waitress?
  Yes, I am.
Are you a waitress at Al's Restaurant?
  Yes, I am.
So, you're... ❞

9a Students A+B

A. Imagine that you are in a clothing store and you each want to buy something. Discuss and decide comparing the items as in the example. Use some of the adjectives in the box.

❝ *I'm looking for a jacket. What do you think of these jackets here?*
  Well, I like the blue jacket. It's... than the green jacket.
Yes, but it's... I think I like the... jacket.
  Yes, I think it's nicer, too. Now, I'm looking for... ❞

nice	modern
beautiful	warm
ugly	casual
long	formal
short	

B. Now that you have both decided what you want to buy, talk with the salesperson (Student C). Use some of the phrases in the box.

Excuse me, I'd like...
What size is this / are these?
I wear a size...
Do you have a large, etc.?
I need a smaller/bigger size.
How much is/are...?
I'll take it/them.
Thank you very much.

2c Pair work Guessing game
Talk in pairs. Try to guess what the objects are.

66 *What's this/that?*
    I don't know. I think it's a...
No, you're wrong. 99

66 *What are these/those?*
    I think they are...
You're right. 99

2b Pair work

Talk in pairs. Look at the people below and give your opinion.

❝ *I like Mark's laptop. I think it's nice.*
Yes, it has a big screen. ❞

9a Student C

B. Imagine that you are a salesperson in a clothing store. Look at the items below and talk with the customers (Students A + B) using some of the phrases in the box.

Can I help you?	Here's a large, etc.
What can I do for you?	Anything else?
What size would you like?	That's... dollars and.... cents, please.
What size do you wear?	Have a nice day!

4b Group work

8c Student A
Guessing game

> *He was born... He died... He was (from)...*
> *He was a/an... He wrote/directed/explored/painted, etc.*

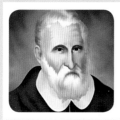

Marco Polo (1254-1324)

- Italian
- explorer and writer
- explored China
- wrote a travel book about China and other countries in Asia

Katsushika Hokusai (1760-1849)

- Japanese
- artist
- famous painting: *The Great Wave*

William Shakespeare (1564-1616)

- English
- poet and writer
- famous play: *Hamlet*

Charlie Chaplin (1889-1977)

- British (but lived in America)
- actor and director
- famous movies: *The Gold Rush, Modern Times*

Alfred Hitchcock (1899-1980)

- British
- director
- famous movies: *Vertigo, The Birds*

Mark Twain (1835-1910)

- American
- writer
- famous books: *Tom Sawyer, Huckleberry Finn*

David Livingstone (1813-1873)

- British
- explorer
- explored Africa

Claude Monet (1840-1926)

- French
- artist
- famous painting: *Water Lilies*

Module 1
The verb *to be*

Affirmative		Negative	
Full Forms	**Short Forms**	**Full Forms**	**Short Forms**
I am	I'm	I am not	I'm not
You are	You're	You are not	You aren't
He is	He's	He is not	He isn't
She is	She's	She is not	She isn't
It is	It's	It is not	It isn't
We are	We're	We are not	We aren't
You are	You're	You are not	You aren't
They are	They're	They are not	They aren't

Questions	Short answers	
Am I?	Yes, I am.	No, I'm not.
Are you?	Yes, you are.	No, you aren't.
Is he?	Yes, he is.	No, he isn't.
Is she?	Yes, she is.	No, she isn't.
Is it?	Yes, it is.	No, it isn't.
Are we?	Yes, we are.	No, we aren't.
Are you?	Yes, you are.	No, you aren't.
Are they?	Yes, they are.	No, they aren't.

I'm not a teacher. I'm a police officer.
• We use short forms when we speak and full forms when we write.

Possessive Adjectives

Personal Pronouns	Possessive Adjectives
I	my
you	your
he	his
she	her
it	its
we	our
you	your
they	their

• **Possessive Adjectives** go before nouns, without articles.
She is my friend. Her name is Emma.

Module 2
The verb *to have*

Affirmative
I have
You have
He has
She has
It has
We have
You have
They have

We use the verb **to have**:
• to express possession.
  I have a blue pen.
  I have two brothers.
• to describe people, animals and things.
  Mary has blond hair.

Possessive Case

• We use the **possessive case** to express possession.
We form the possessive case by adding 's to a singular noun.
This is Tom's book.
This is my sister's pencil.

Adjectives

• We use adjectives **before nouns** and **after the verb** *to be*.
  That's a beautiful camera.   *That camera is beautiful.*
• Adjectives are the same in singular and in plural.
  I have a new folder.   *I have new folders.*

this/that - these/those

Singular	Plural
this	these
that	those

• We use **this/these** to point out people, animals or things that are close to us.
  This is my pen.   *These are my pens.*
• We use **that/those** to point out people, animals or things that are far from us.
  That is a book.   *Those are books.*

Plural nouns

Regular nouns
• Most nouns take -s. bag → bags, pen → pens
• Nouns ending in -s, -ch, -sh,-x, -o take -es. class → classes, watch → watches
• Nouns ending in a consonant + y, drop the -y and take -ies. country → countries **But** boy → boys

Irregular nouns		
man	→	men
woman	→	women
child	→	children

Module 3
) Present Simple

Affirmative
I work
You work
He works
She works
It works
We work
You work
They work

Negative	
Full Forms	**Short Forms**
I do not work	I don't work
You do not work	You don't work
He does not work	He doesn't work
She does not work	She doesn't work
It does not work	It doesn't work
We do not work	We don't work
You do not work	You don't work
They do not work	They don't work

Questions	Short answers	
Do I work?	Yes, I do.	No, I don't.
Do you work?	Yes, you do.	No, you don't.
Does he work?	Yes, he does.	No, he doesn't.
Does she work?	Yes, she does.	No, she doesn't.
Does it work?	Yes, it does.	No, it doesn't.
Do we work?	Yes, we do.	No, we don't.
Do you work?	Yes, you do.	No, you don't.
Do they work?	Yes, they do.	No, they don't.

No **-s** in the 3rd person singular after **does/doesn't**.

Formation of the 3rd person singular (he/she/it)

- Most verbs take -s.
  I get → He gets
  I like → He likes
- Verbs ending in -ss, -sh,
  -ch, -x, -o take -es.
  I watch → He watches
  I go → He goes
- Verbs ending in a
  consonant + y, drop the -y
  and take -ies.
  I study → He studies
  But I play → He plays

We use the **Present Simple**:

- for habits or actions that happen regularly.
  I watch TV every day.
  She goes out on the weekend.
- for situations that are always the same.
  We live in Boston.
  I like ice cream.
- for daily schedules.
  She starts work at 8:30 every day.

) Prepositions of time

- **at:** at six o'clock / at two thirty
  at noon / at night / at midnight, etc.
- **in:** in the morning / afternoon / evening
  in my spare time, etc.
- **on:** on Friday / on Mondays, etc.
  on Friday morning
  on weekdays / on the weekend

) Present Simple (Yes/No questions, Wh-questions)

- Questions which start with **Do/Does** have a Yes/No answer.
  A: *Do you like ice cream?*
  B: *Yes, I do. / No, I don't.*
- We use **Who, What, Where, When, etc.** to ask questions and request information.
  A: *When do you go to the movies?*
  B: *On Sundays.*

) Question Words

- **Who? :** We ask about people.
  Who's that? My friend, Kim.
- **What?:** We ask about things, animals and actions.
  What's your favorite sport?
  Basketball.
- **Where?:** We ask about places.
  I'm from Madrid. Where are you from?
- **How?:** We ask about the way in which something happens or to find out someone's news.
  How are things at work?
  Boring, as usual.
- **How old?:** We ask about ages.
  How old are you?
  Twenty-four.
- **When /** We ask about time.
  What time?: *When do you play tennis?*
  On the weekend.
  What time do you finish work?
  At 5:30.
- **Whose?:** We ask about possession.
  Whose book is this?
  It's Mary's.

Module 4
▶ Adverbs of frequency

never	sometimes	often	usually	always

We use **adverbs of frequency** to talk about how often we do something. We place them:

- **before** the main verb.
  John often plays football on Saturdays.
  Peter doesn't always eat breakfast.
- **after** the verb *to be*.
  Sheryl is never late for school.

▶ There is / There are

	Affirmative		Negative	
	Full Forms	Short Forms	Full Forms	Short Forms
Singular	There is	There's	There is not	There isn't
Plural	There are	><	There are not	There aren't

	Questions	Short answers	
Singular	Is there...?	Yes, there is.	No, there isn't.
Plural	Are there...?	Yes, there are.	No, there aren't.

- We use **there is** before singular nouns.
  There's a bedroom downstairs.
- We use **there are** before plural nouns.
  Are there two armchairs in the room?

▶ Articles: *a(n)* vs. *the*

a/an + singular nouns
- when we mention something for the first time
  There's a microwave in the kitchen.
- when we talk about jobs
  He's a doctor.

no a/an before plural nouns
Cats are great pets.

the + singular or plural nouns
- when we talk about something specific
  There are two boys outside. The tall boy is Kevin.
- when we talk about something unique
  The sun is hot.

no articles
- before possessive adjectives
  My cat is white.
- before proper nouns
  Fiona is thirteen years old.
  Madrid is in Spain.
- when we talk about something in general
  Dogs are friendly animals.

Module 5
▶ The verb *can*

Affirmative	Negative	
	Full Forms	Short Forms
I can dance	I cannot dance	I can't dance
You can dance	You cannot dance	You can't dance
He can dance	He cannot dance	He can't dance
She can dance	She cannot dance	She can't dance
It can dance	It cannot dance	It can't dance
We can dance	We cannot dance	We can't dance
You can dance	You cannot dance	You can't dance
They can dance	They cannot dance	They can't dance

Questions	Short answers	
Can I dance?	Yes, I can.	No, I can't.
Can you dance?	Yes, you can.	No, you can't.
Can he dance?	Yes, he can.	No, he can't.
Can she dance?	Yes, she can.	No, she can't.
Can it dance?	Yes, it can.	No, it can't.
Can we dance?	Yes, we can.	No, we can't.
Can you dance?	Yes, you can.	No, you can't.
Can they dance?	Yes, they can.	No, they can't.

We use **can** to express ability: *He can swim.*

The verb **can** is a modal verb. It doesn't take an *-s* in the third person singular, it doesn't form the negative and question form with *do/does*, and it is always followed by the base form of the verb.

▶ Imperative

Affirmative	Listen to the CD.	Be quiet!
Negative	Don't close your books.	Don't be late.

- We can use **please** to be more polite.
  Speak in English, please!

▶ Object Personal Pronouns

Personal Pronouns	
subject	object
I	me
you	you
he	him
she	her
it	it
we	us
you	you
they	them

- **Subject personal pronouns** are used as subjects and go before the verb.
  Look at that girl. She's beautiful!
- **Object personal pronouns** are used after verbs as objects or after prepositions.
  Look at that boy. Do you know him?
  That woman is looking at us.

Module 6

Countable and Uncountable nouns

- **Countable nouns** have both a singular and a plural form and we can count them. We use *a/an* and numbers before countable nouns.
  a table - two tables

- **Uncountable nouns** only have a singular form and we cannot count them.
  cheese - meat - milk

- We don't use *a/an* or numbers before uncountable nouns but we often use *some* and *any*.
  A: *Is there any milk?*
  B: *No, but there's some yogurt.*

	Singular	**Plural**
Countable nouns	a carrot	carrots
Uncountable nouns	milk	✕

Some / Any

- **some + uncountable / plural countable nouns** in affirmative sentences and offers.
  There is some orange juice in the refrigerator.
  Would you like some fries?

- **any + uncountable / plural countable nouns** in questions and negative sentences.
  Is there any orange juice in the refrigerator?
  There aren't any potato chips on the table.

How much...? / How many...?

- We use **How much...?** with uncountable nouns to ask about the quantity of something.
  How much water is in the bottle?

- We use **How many...?** with plural countable nouns to ask about the number of something.
  How many students are there in the classroom?

Module 7

Present Progressive

Affirmative	
Full Forms	**Short Forms**
I am playing	I'm playing
You are playing	You're playing
He is playing	He's playing
She is playing	She's playing
It is playing	It's playing
We are playing	We're playing
You are playing	You're playing
They are playing	They're playing

Negative	
Full Forms	**Short Forms**
I am not playing	I'm not playing
You are not playing	You aren't playing
He is not playing	He isn't playing
She is not playing	She isn't playing
It is not playing	It isn't playing
We are not playing	We aren't playing
You are not playing	You aren't playing
They are not playing	They aren't playing

Questions	Short answers	
Am I playing?	Yes, I am.	No, I'm not.
Are you playing?	Yes, you are.	No, you aren't.
Is he playing?	Yes, he is.	No, he isn't.
Is she playing?	Yes, she is.	No, she isn't.
Is it playing?	Yes, it is.	No, it isn't.
Are we playing?	Yes, we are.	No, we aren't.
Are you playing?	Yes, you are.	No, you aren't.
Are they playing?	Yes, they are.	No, they aren't.

- We use the **Present Progressive** for actions that are happening at the moment of speaking.
  What is Kelly doing now?   She's talking on the phone.

Formation of *-ing*

Most verbs take *-ing*.   *talk → talking*
Verbs ending in *-e*, drop the *-e* before the *-ing*. *come → coming*
Verbs with one syllable ending in one vowel + one consonant, double the consonant before the *-ing*. *stop → stopping*
Verbs with two or more syllables ending in one stressed vowel + one consonant, double the consonant before the *-ing*. *begin → beginning*   **But**   *answer → answering*
Verbs ending in a stressed syllable +*-l*, double the *-l* before the *-ing*. *propel → propelling*   **But**   *travel → traveling*
Verbs ending in *-ie* take *-ying*.   *die → dying*

TIME EXPRESSIONS
now, right now

Module 8

- We use the **Past Simple** to talk about things that happened in the past.
I visited Carla yesterday.

Past Simple of regular verbs (Affirmative)

Affirmative
I / You / He / She / It / We / You / They played

Spelling	
Most verbs take -ed.	start → started
Verbs ending in -e, take -d.	dance → danced
Verbs ending in a consonant + -y, take -ied.	try → tried **But** play → played
Verbs with one syllable ending in one vowel + one consonant, double the consonant before the -ed.	stop → stopped
Verbs with two or more syllables ending in a stressed vowel + one consonant, double the consonant before the -ed.	prefer → preferred **But** answer → answered
Verbs ending in a stressed syllable + -l, double the -l before the -ed.	propel → propelled **But** travel → traveled

Past Simple of irregular verbs (Affirmative)

- Irregular verbs don't take -ed in the Past Simple.

Affirmative
I / You / He / She / It / We / You / They (go →) went

Look at the list of irregular verbs on page 117.

TIME EXPRESSIONS
yesterday / yesterday morning, etc. in + years / centuries last night / week / month / year last Wednesday / Friday, etc. last summer / winter, etc. two days / a week / three months ago

Past Simple

Affirmative	Negative	
	Full Forms	Short Forms
I liked/ate	I did not like/eat	I didn't like/eat
You liked/ate	You did not like/eat	You didn't like/eat
He liked/ate	He did not like/eat	He didn't like/eat
She liked/ate	She did not like/eat	She didn't like/eat
It liked/ate	It did not like/eat	It didn't like/eat
We liked/ate	We did not like/eat	We didn't like/eat
You liked/ate	You did not like/eat	You didn't like/eat
They liked/ate	They did not like/eat	They didn't like/eat

Questions	Short answers	
Did I like/eat?	Yes, I did.	No, I didn't.
Did you like/eat?	Yes, you did.	No, you didn't.
Did he like/eat?	Yes, he did.	No, he didn't.
Did she like/eat?	Yes, she did.	No, she didn't.
Did it like/eat?	Yes, it did.	No, it didn't.
Did we like/eat?	Yes, we did.	No, we didn't.
Did you like/eat?	Yes, you did.	No, you didn't.
Did they like/eat?	Yes, they did.	No, they didn't.

Past Simple (Yes/No questions, Wh-questions)

- Questions which start with **Did** have a Yes/No answer.
  A: *Did you go to Charlie's house last night?*
  B: *Yes, I did. / No, I didn't.*

- We use **Who, What, Where, When, etc.** to ask questions and request information.
  A: *What did you do last night?*
  B: *I stayed home.*

Past Simple of *to be*

Affirmative	Negative	
	Full Forms	Short Forms
I was	I was not	I wasn't
You were	You were not	You weren't
He was	He was not	He wasn't
She was	She was not	She wasn't
It was	It was not	It wasn't
We were	We were not	We weren't
You were	You were not	You weren't
They were	They were not	They weren't

Questions	Short answers	
Was I?	Yes, I was.	No, I wasn't.
Were you?	Yes, you were.	No, you weren't.
Was he?	Yes, he was.	No, he wasn't.
Was she?	Yes, she was.	No, she wasn't.
Was it?	Yes, it was.	No, it wasn't.
Were we?	Yes, we were.	No, we weren't.
Were you?	Yes, you were.	No, you weren't.
Were they?	Yes, they were.	No, they weren't.

There was / There were

Affirmative	Negative
There was	There wasn't
There were	There weren't

Questions	Short Answers
Was there?	Yes, there was. No, there wasn't.
Were there?	Yes, there were. No, there weren't.

Module 9

) Comparative and Superlative forms

- We use the **comparative** of adjectives when we compare two people, animals or things.

- We use the **superlative** of adjectives when we compare one person, animal or thing with several of the same kind.

Formation
Comparative: adjective + -er / more + adjective } + than
John is older than Peter. *My watch is more expensive than yours.*
Superlative: the + adjective + -est / most + adjective } + of / in
John is the oldest boy in his class. *This watch is the most expensive of all.*

All one-syllable and most two-syllable adjectives take -er / -est.	short - shorter - shortest
One-syllable adjectives ending in -e take -r / -st.	safe - safer - safest
One-syllable adjectives ending in one vowel + one consonant, double the consonant before the -er / -est.	big - bigger - biggest
Adjectives ending in a consonant + -y, drop the -y and take -ier /-iest.	easy - easier - easiest
Adjectives with three or more syllables and some two-syllable adjectives take more + adjective / most + adjective.	dangerous - more dangerous - most dangerous

Irregular forms		
Positive Form	**Comparative form**	**Superlative form**
good	better	the best
bad	worse	the worst
far	farther further	the farthest the furthest

Module 10

) Future *going to*

Affirmative	
Full Forms	**Short Forms**
I am going to work	I'm going to work
You are going to work	You're going to work
He is going to work	He's going to work
She is going to work	She's going to work
It is going to work	It's going to work
We are going to work	We're going to work
You are going to work	You're going to work
They are going to work	They're going to work

Negative	
Full Forms	**Short Forms**
I am not going to work	I'm not going to work
You are not going to work	You aren't going to work
He is not going to work	He isn't going to work
She is not going to work	She isn't going to work
It is not going to work	It isn't going to work
We are not going to work	We aren't going to work
You are not going to work	You aren't going to work
They are not going to work	They aren't going to work

Questions	Short answers	
Am I going to work?	Yes, I am.	No, I'm not.
Are you going to work?	Yes, you are.	No, you aren't.
Is he going to work?	Yes, he is.	No, he isn't.
Is she going to work?	Yes, she is.	No, she isn't.
Is it going to work?	Yes, it is.	No, it isn't.
Are we going to work?	Yes, we are.	No, we aren't.
Are you going to work?	Yes, you are.	No, you aren't.
Are they going to work?	Yes, they are.	No, they aren't.

We use the **Future *going to*** to express future plans.
Ben is going to buy a car next week.

TIME EXPRESSIONS
tomorrow, tonight, soon next week/month/Monday, etc. in an hour/a year, etc. this week/month, etc.

> It isn't necessary to say or write **to go** with the Future *going to*.
> *Ted's going (to go) swimming next week.*

) The verb *should*

Affirmative
I / You / He / She / It / We / You / They   should go

Negative
I / You / He / She / It / We / You / They   shouldn't go

Questions
Should   I / you / he / she / it / we / you / they   go?

We use **should**:
- to ask for and give advice.
  What should I do? You shouldn't work so hard.

- to express an opinion.
  I think the children should eat more fruit.

- to make a suggestion.
  We should go to the movies. There's a nice movie playing.

Base form	Past Simple	Base form	Past Simple
be	was/were	leave	left
become	became	lend	lent
begin	began	let	let
break	broke	lie	lay
bring	brought	lose	lost
build	built	make	made
buy	bought	mean	meant
catch	caught	meet	met
choose	chose	pay	paid
come	came	put	put
cost	cost	read	read
cut	cut	ride	rode
do	did	ring	rang
draw	drew	run	ran
drink	drank	say	said
drive	drove	see	saw
eat	ate	sell	sold
fall	fell	send	sent
feed	fed	sing	sang
feel	felt	sit	sat
fight	fought	sleep	slept
find	found	speak	spoke
fly	flew	spend	spent
forget	forgot	stand	stood
get	got	steal	stole
give	gave	swim	swam
go	went	take	took
grow	grew	teach	taught
hang	hung	tell	told
have	had	think	thought
hear	heard	throw	threw
hide	hid	understand	understood
hit	hit	wake	woke
hold	held	wear	wore
hurt	hurt	win	won
keep	kept	write	wrote
know	knew		

In class: How to learn better in class

- Look at the board and take notes.
- Listen carefully to your teacher and the CD.
- Ask your teacher when you don't understand.
- Speak in English as much as possible.
- Take part in pair and group work activities.

Outside the class: How to learn better outside the class

- Read the dialogues and texts from your book and listen to them.
- Read the dialogues and texts aloud and sometimes record yourself.
- Study the vocabulary and grammar and then do your homework.
- Read selected texts from magazines and newspapers in English.
- Read websites in English.
- Listen to songs in English.
- Watch TV shows and DVDs in English.

Vocabulary: How to learn vocabulary better

- Write down new words in a notebook.
  Together with the English word:
  - write the translation in your language
  - write an example sentence.
- Put words in groups or use diagrams.
- Learn whole phrases (eg. verb+noun) not just isolated words.
- Learn new words in context (in sentences describing situations). This way, it is easier to remember them.
- When you learn new words, you must remember if they are verbs, nouns, adjectives, etc.
- When you learn new words, it's a good idea to learn any synonyms and/or opposites.
- Some words are very similar in meaning and can easily be confused. Try to remember the context where they are usually used.

- Pay attention to cognates and false friends.
  Cognates are English words which are similar in form and meaning to words in your language. False friends are English words which have a similar form to words in your language, but they have a different meaning.
- Refer to the Word List.
- Practice the spelling and pronunciation of new words.
- Look up unknown words in a dictionary. There, you can find a lot of useful information about a word: pronunciation, word class (noun, verb, etc.), meaning and example sentences.
- Regularly revise words you have learned.
- Try to use words you have recently learned when you speak or write.

Grammar: How to learn grammar better

- Refer to the Grammar Reference.
- Use grammar tables.
- Have a grammar notebook. In it write:
  - tips and/or rules in your language
  - example sentences
  - important grammatical points e.g. irregular verbs.
- Make a note of grammatical errors that you often make.

Speak: How to do better when doing speaking tasks

- Before you speak, make sure you understand the task and how you should use the prompts.
- Look at the example and use the prompts given.
- Use the language you have learned.
- Speak only in English.
- Speak clearly.
- Don't worry if you make a mistake. Correct yourself if you can, otherwise continue speaking.
- If you can't remember a word, don't stop. Try to use other words.

- When answering open-ended questions, don't use one-word answers. Try to express an opinion and justify your answers using examples.
- When talking to another person, listen carefully to him/her and respond to what he/she is saying (e.g. *That's great news! How awful!*). Also, show interest or surprise by using phrases like *Really?, Did you?,* etc. and try to keep the conversation going.
- Keep in mind that your tone of voice can help enhance what you are saying. You can show concern, sympathize, etc.

Read: How to do better when doing reading tasks

- Before you read, try to predict what the text is about with the help of the title and the pictures.
- Look for key words in the text to understand the main ideas.
- Try to understand which of the words in the text are really important. Try to guess the meaning of as many of these words as possible from the context.
- Read the text quickly to understand the main idea.
- Read the text carefully to understand specific details.

- Read the whole text before you do an exercise. Sometimes the answers require overall understanding.
- Decide in which part of the text you can find the information you need.
- Make sure you understand who or what the pronouns (he, it, this, them, etc.) and the adverbs (here, there, etc.) refer to in the text.

Listen: How to do better when doing listening tasks

- Before you listen, read the rubric carefully and look at the pictures. Try to predict what the speakers are going to talk about.
- Before you listen, read the statements or questions carefully. This will give you an idea of what to listen for.
- While listening for gist, try to understand the general idea, not every single word.
- Listen for key words to understand the main ideas.
- While listening, don't assume that an answer is correct just because the speakers mention a word that is in the activity. Listen carefully before you answer.

- When completing sentences, make sure that your answers make sense with the rest of the sentence.
- Don't be in a hurry to answer a multiple choice question. Listen carefully till the end and check all the options before your final decision.
- Pay attention to the speakers' tone of voice to understand how they are feeling.

Write: How to do better when doing writing tasks

- Make sure you write what the rubric asks you to. Don't include irrelevant information.
- Before you start, plan your writing. Think about the topic carefully and try to come up with ideas which are relevant to it. Make notes of the information you want to include.
- Use linking words (*and, but, so, because, first, then,* etc.) to join your ideas and make your writing flow.

- Use words like *he, she, it, them,* etc. to avoid repeating the same words.
- When you are asked to write a letter, remember to use set phrases.
- Write neatly.
- Write your first draft and correct it. Then write your final draft.
- Edit your writing. Check punctuation, capital letters, word order, spelling, grammar, vocabulary and linking words.

spelling

American English	British English
airplane	aeroplane
center	centre
color	colour
cozy	cosy
favorite	favourite
gray	grey
meter	metre
neighbor	neighbour
neighborhood	neighbourhood
omelet	omelette
organization	organisation
organize	organise
percent	per cent
practice (v)	practise
story (of a building)	storey (of a building)
theater	theatre
traveler	traveller

grammar and usage

American English	British English
January 16th	16th January
do well on	do well in
on the team	in the team
on the weekend	at the weekend
learned	learnt, learned
spelled	spelt, spelled

words and phrases

American English	British English
across from	opposite
apartment	flat
apartment building	block of flats
baked potato	jacket potato
bill	note
blond (hair)	fair (hair)
campground	campsite
candy	sweets
carry-on	hand luggage
cell	mobile
check	tick
closet	wardrobe
coffee shop	café
cookie	biscuit
couch	sofa
do/wash the dishes	do the washing-up
do the laundry	do the washing
doctor's office	doctor's surgery
downtown (area)	city centre
elementary school	primary school
elevator	lift
fall	autumn
faucet	tap
flashlight	torch
(French) fries	chips
gas	petrol
give somebody a ride	give somebody a lift
go grocery shopping	do the shopping
go to the movies	go to the cinema
grade	mark
gym	PE
high school	secondary school
highway	motorway
last name	surname
mad	angry
Math	Maths
mom	mum
motorcycle	motorbike
movie	film
movie theater	cinema
pants	trousers
parentheses	brackets
parking lot	car park
period	full stop
ping-pong	table tennis
potato chips	crisps
purse	handbag
refrigerator	fridge
roommate	flatmate
salesperson	shop assistant
Science major	Science student
sick	ill
sidewalk	pavement
sneakers	trainers
soccer	football
soda	soft drink
store	shop
stove, oven	cooker
subway	underground
sweater	jumper
take a shower	have a shower
talk show	chat show
the check	the bill
track and field	athletics
trash, garbage	rubbish
trash/garbage can	rubbish bin
vacation	holiday
vacuum	hoover
yard	garden
zip code	post code

Vowel sounds

/iː/ read	/ɪ/ did	/ɛ/ next	/æ/ back
/ɑː/ bottle	/ɔː/ boring	/ʊ/ good	/uː/ food
/ʌ/ butter	/ɜː/ bird	/ə/ father	/eɪ/ player
/oʊ/ boat	/aɪ/ nine	/aʊ/ about	/ɔɪ/ point

Consonant sounds

/p/ pet	/b/ book	/d/ doctor	/k/ kid	/g/ grandson	/tʃ/ chair
/dʒ/ large	/f/ first	/v/ vet	/θ/ theater	/ð/ that	/s/ space
/z/ has	/t/ take	/ʃ/ shop	/ʒ/ usually	/h/ whole	/m/ man
/n/ neat	/ŋ/ thing	/w/ wear	/l/ lips	/r/ room	/j/ yellow

Module 1

1a

1. Good afternoon.
2. Hello, how are you?
3. See you later!
4. Take care.
5. Hello. What's your name?
6. Nice to meet you.
7. Mark, this is Mary.
8. What's up?

1c

1.

A: Hi, Gary.

B: Hello, Mary. What's up?

A: Not much. Hey, is your neighbor an electrician?

B: No, she's an architect.

A: Oh.

2.

A: OK ma'am. What's your phone number?

B: It's 199-443-4545.

A: 199-443-4545. Great. Thank you.

3.

A: And what's his number?

B: I don't know. But I know his e-mail.
It's ryan@blackdent.com.

A: Thanks.

1d

B.

A: Good morning. Can I ask you some questions for this form?

B: Sure.

A: What's your first name?

B: Jon. But, it's J-O-N.

A: I see, no H.

B: That's right.

A: And your last name?

B: It's Davies.

A: Is that D-A-V-I-S?

B: No, it's D-A-V-I-E-S.

C.

A: OK, Mr. Davies. How old are you?

B: I'm 34.

A: And where are you from?

B: Well, I'm American, but I live in Australia.

A: So, you're from the U.S.A.

B: Yes, that's right.

A: And what do you do?

B: I'm a doctor.

A: OK. Now, what's your phone number?

B: Well, my home number is 221-554-8988.

A: 554...?

B: 8988.

A: Great. What's your cell number?

B: Hmm. Let me think... It's 244-575-5998.

A: ... 5998. One more thing. What's your e-mail address?

B: It's jd445@gmail.com.

A: OK, thank you. That's all I need for now.

Module 2

2b

1.

A: Nice phone, Roy.

B: Thanks. It's new.

A: My brother has the same phone. His is white, too.

B: Yeah, black phones are OK, but I think white phones are awesome.

A: Me too.

2.

A: Is that your tablet, Wendy?

B: Yes, it is.

A: It's really nice. Is it new?

B: No, not really. It's old.

A: I want a tablet, too.

3.

A: Hey, look at that laptop!

B: Where?

A: Over there. Look, it's very cheap.

B: No, it isn't. Look at the zeros.

A: Oh, yes. It is expensive. Silly me!

A: Excuse me, ma'am. Can you open your bag, please?

B: Sure. Let me see. I have my laptop and my cell phone.

A: What's this?

B: That's my umbrella.

A: Oh, it's very small.

B: I also have my keys.

A: Are these your sunglasses?

B: Yes, they are.

A: OK, that's fine. You can put them back now. Have a nice flight!

B: Thanks.

A: Hey, Steve. Take this to Mr. Dupont for me, please.

B: Of course, Mr. Blake. Umm... Who's Mr. Dupont again?

A: The new French teacher.

B: The new French teacher? Umm... Is he chubby?

A: No, he's tall and slim.

B: He has short dark hair, right?

A: No, he has short gray hair.

B: I think I know Mr. Dupont. He's young, right?

A: Well, not that young. He's middle-aged.

B: OK, I'll find him.

A: Thanks Steve.

Module 3

1.

A: Do you like soccer?

B: No, I don't. I think it's boring.

A: I really like soccer. I watch the soccer final every year.

B: Do you play soccer a lot?

A: No, I don't play at all. I just watch it on TV.

B: I see.

2.

A: Do you like sports, Fred?

B: Well, I like cycling very much.

A: Really? I like cycling, too. Let's go cycling together. I go every evening after work.

B: I don't. I don't have time. I go on the weekend.

A: Oh, I see.

3.

A: Let's play ping-pong today.

B: Oh, no, not again.

A: Come on, it's fun!

B: No, it isn't. I hate it. Hey, let's watch tennis on TV today.

A: TV's boring!

B: Yeah, you're right.

A: I have an idea! Let's go to the park and play tennis.

B: OK, it's a change from ping-pong.

A: Excuse me, can I ask you some questions for a survey?

B: Sure.

A: Thanks. How old are you?

B: I'm 26.

A: OK, do you have a lot of spare time?

B: No, I don't. I'm a college student, and I study a lot.

A: What do you do in your spare time?

B: Umm... I like sports and I hang out with my friends.

A: Anything else?

B: Umm... I don't like video games, but I read magazines a lot.

A: OK. What about your favorite spare-time activity?

B: I love the gym. I go there every day.

A: On the weekend, too?

B: No, just on weekdays.

A: I see. And who do you go there with?

B: My friends from college. They love going to the gym, too.

A: Great. That's all, thank you.

1.

A: Welcome back. So, Gary, here's your next question for 100 dollars. What is basketball star Michael Jordan's middle name?

B: Jeffrey!

A: That's right! Well done. OK, now for your last question...

2.

A: Hey, Julie. What's on?

B: Not much. Do you like documentaries?

A: Not really. What's it about?

B: Doctors around the world.

A: Boring! Let's check the other channels... Soccer! Yes!

B: Oh no! See you later.

3.

A: Oh no! It's 6 o'clock.

B: What's wrong, Kim?

A: Where's your TV?

B: Do you watch that soap opera every day? It's really bad, you know.

A: No, the news is on at 6. And I watch that every day.

B: Oh, I see.

Module 4

4a

A: Excuse me. Can I ask you some questions for a survey?

B: Sure. What's it about?

A: Housework.

B: OK.

A: Do you live alone?

B: No, I'm married.

A: OK. Who usually does the dishes in your house?

B: I always do the dishes.

A: After every meal?

B: Yes, breakfast, lunch and dinner. You see, I don't work.

A: And do you vacuum, too?

B: Yes, I do. Mark hates vacuuming but he does other jobs.

A: Like what?

B: Well, he washes the car every week, usually on Sundays.

A: I see. Anything else? Does he do the laundry?

B: No, I do that. It's my favorite job around the house.

A: What about the grocery shopping?

B: Well, Mark and I always go grocery shopping together on Thursday evenings.

A: I see. Thanks for your time.

B: No problem.

4c

A: So, what do you think, Ryan?

B: I don't know. I like both apartments.

A: Me too. There is only one bedroom in this apartment. Is that a problem?

B: No, it's a large bedroom, and the living room is really big, too.

A: What about the balcony? The other apartment has two.

B: Yes, but they're small. This apartment has a really big balcony.

A: You're right, but there's a small kitchen.

B: We don't cook a lot, anyway. Let's rent it.

A: OK, then. Great! I love big balconies.

B: Me too.

4d

1.

A: Hi, Elisa. What's your new place like?

B: It's great. It has two bedrooms and a large bathroom.

A: Is there a big living room?

B: No, it's pretty small.

A: Do you have a backyard?

B: Umm, I live on the 10th floor, you know.

A: Of course. Sorry.

2.

A: Hey, Gary. Where do you live?

B: In Springfield.

A: I know that. What's your address?

B: Oh, it's 365 Lockwood Street.

A: Great.

B: Why?

A: I want to send you a postcard when I go on vacation.

B: I see.

Module 5

5a

A: And now over to you Greg, our "eye in the sky" in the helicopter. What's the city like today, Greg?

B: Well, it's not too bad. As you know, there's a bicycle race downtown today, so it isn't a normal day. There's no shopping because all the stores are closed. But it's a beautiful day and there are people all over the city. Main Street is closed, so there are no cars at all down there. However, I can see lots of cars and buses stuck on Park Avenue. I don't know what the problem is, but I'm sure there are lots of drivers and people that aren't happy on those buses. As I say, it's a beautiful day, so I think the best idea is to take the subway downtown and then walk around the city. Let's look at a few more streets around the city...

5b

1.

A: Sorry, but I'm not from around here. How do I get there?

B: It's easy. It's only a five-minute walk. Go down this street and turn left at the gas station. Go straight again and at the traffic lights turn right. It's on your left, next to a bank.

2.

A: Sorry, where is it again?

B: Go down this road and turn right at the park. Then go straight and turn left at the traffic lights. That's Elm Street.

A: Is it on Elm Street?

B: Yes, it's between the movie theater and the bank.

A: Great. Thank you.

3.

A: That's great, but how can I get there? Is it far?

B: It's not far. Go down this street and turn left at the supermarket. Go straight. Then turn right at the movie theater. I think that's Bell Road. Go straight for a while and it's on your right. It's across from a restaurant.

A: Thanks.

B: No problem.

1.

Girl Wow! That actor is awesome!

Boy Yeah, this is a great play.

Man Excuse me, can you sit down, please?

Boy Tina, sit down. The other people can't see.

Girl Oh, sorry.

2.

A: Two tickets, please.

B: We have a special offer. $30 for visits to both this museum and Fenwick Castle.

A: Where's that?

B: On the other side of the city, near Fenwick Park.

A: No, we don't have time for that today. We just want to see the paintings from South American artists.

3.

A: So, what do you think, Mike?

B: This is really awesome.

A: Yep. The Bears are a great team.

B: Do you want to go for coffee after the game?

A: No, I need to get home early.

B: OK.

4.

A: Come on, let's go for coffee. I'm tired.

B: But there's more to see.

A: I know but we have time.

B: What about the kids?

A: Let them walk around and look at the fish for a while. It isn't dangerous in here.

Module 6

Waiter What would you like to order?

Man Sandra?

Woman I'd like a cheese and cucumber sandwich, please.

Waiter A sandwich for you, too?

Man No. I'd like three tacos.

Waiter Very well, sir.

Man And I also want some fries.

Waiter What would you like to drink?

Man Some pineapple juice, please.

Woman Just some water for me.

Waiter Great. Anything for dessert?

Man Not for me. I'm on a diet. Sandra?

Woman I'd like some ice cream.

Waiter The vanilla ice cream is very nice.

Woman No, my favorite is banana.

Waiter OK, then. Is that all?

Man I'd like to try some vanilla ice cream with some carrot cake.

Woman Alan! What about your diet?

Man OK, OK. I don't want any dessert, thank you.

Waiter Would you like your drinks now, or would you...

Kelly

Oh, a lot. I get up early in the morning so I need two cups, at least. Then I have another cup at about eleven, and I also have a cup after lunch, too.

Debbie

I don't eat a lot. You see, I don't really like them. My roommate often makes some, but I like cake, especially chocolate cake.

Robert

I usually drink three or four bottles. I exercise every day and I get very thirsty, you see.

Simon

I don't really know. Umm... We don't have them in the house. But I sometimes buy a bag to have for lunch at work, with my sandwich and fruit.

1.

A: Hey Ian. What's that? Cereal?

B: Yeah, I'm hungry.

A: People usually eat cereal for breakfast, you know.

B: Not me. I like it in the evening.

A: What do you have for breakfast? An omelet?

B: No, I just have a cup of coffee and some toast.

A: That's why you're hungry all day.

B: Maybe.

2.

A: What's up, Kelly?

B: Hey, I know a great restaurant on 10th Avenue. I go there every Friday night and they have amazing goulash. Do you want to come?

A: Goulash? What's that?

B: It's a meat and vegetable soup, with lots of paprika.

A: No, I don't like Mexican food.

B: It's not Mexican. It's Hungarian.

A: No thanks. I like Italian food. I can eat pizza or pasta every day of the week.

B: Suit yourself.

Module 7

7b

1.

A: Hey Richard.

B: What's up, Ken? What are you doing there?

A: I'm trying to charge my MP3 player.

B: Need any help?

A: Yes, please. This is the right charger, right?

B: Yeah, but I think you need to turn it on to charge it.

A: Really?

B: Yes, look. There you go.

A: Thanks a lot.

B: Don't mention it.

2.

A: Hi, Natalie.

B: Hi there, Jenny.

A: Are you working on your English assignment?

B: No, I'm not. I'm downloading some songs.

A: Anything good?

B: Yeah, I think so. Jenny, I want to put them on my tablet, but I don't know how. Can you help me?

A: I'm afraid I don't know about tablets. My brother does, though. Maybe I can ask him.

B: No, it's OK. Thanks anyway.

7c

A: Welcome back, so now it's time for the answers to our computer quiz.

B: That's right, Steve. The first question is about the Internet country code .ch.

A: Yeah, a lot of people think that .ch stands for China, but it doesn't.

B: No?

A: It's actually the code for Switzerland. Now, the next question is about megabytes, gigabytes, and terabytes.

B: Yes. A terabyte is 1,000 gigabytes, but what is a thousand terabytes? Is it an ultrabyte?

A: No, and it isn't a zettabyte, either. So, the answer is a petabyte.

B: OK. What's the next question?

A: This one is simple. What does .edu stand for at the end of a web address?

B: Education, right? It's used for schools and colleges, etc.

A: You're right. Next question: What is QWERTY?

B: I have no idea. It sounds like a made-up word.

A: Well, you have a laptop in front of you. Look at the first five letters.

B: Q... W... E... I see! Good question.

A: Last one. Don't look at your keyboard for this one. Where does the arrow point to on the "ENTER" key?

B: I don't remember... I don't think it's up, so I'm guessing... to the right?

A: No, it's to the left.

B: Oh, yes. So it is. Well, next week we will have...

7d

1.

A: Hello?

B: Hi, Simon. How's it going?

A: Not too bad. Where are you?

B: I'm in Miami.

A: Lucky guy. What's it like there?

B: Nice and sunny, as usual. What about New York?

A: Don't ask.

B: Is it raining, again?

A: Yeah, every day for a week, now.

B: Well, at least it isn't snowing.

A: That's true.

2.

A: Hey, let's go out tonight.

B: No, it's cold. Let's stay home.

A: Come on, there's a great new restaurant on Greenford Avenue.

B: No, thanks. I'm not hungry.

A: Well, you're a lot of fun to be around.

B: OK, how about going to the new movie theater on Madison Road? I want to watch *Metal Man 2*.

A: Really? Me too.

B: Great. Come on.

3.

A: Let me see. Is that the weather for this week?

B: Yeah, it doesn't look good.

A: But I want to go to the beach on Thursday.

B: Not a good idea. Just stay in and watch TV all day.

A: Does that site have the weather for the weekend?

B: Yeah, let me see... There!

A: That's better. I can go on Saturday, then. Great! How about coming with me?

Module 8

1.

A: Hey, check out these photos.

B: Is that you, Tony?

A: Yeah, it's my first year in High School.

B: When did you enter High School?

A: 1994, I think. Yes, that's right.

B: So, you graduated in 1999?

A: No, look at the year book. Class of 98!

B: Oh yeah.

2.

A: Hey Dora, your mom's a teacher, right?

B: Yeah, she teaches Physics at Rowland High School.

A: So, why did you choose to study History at college? Didn't you like Physics?

B: Well, I did, but I had an amazing History teacher at school. She made everything very interesting. So, I started loving that subject.

A: But, you didn't want to become a teacher?

B: No, I always wanted to have my own coffee shop.

A: I see.

3.

A: Did you have a favorite subject at school?

B: Not really. I liked Art, I suppose.

A: Who did you have for Art?

B: Mr. Jenkins. All the kids really liked him.

A: I didn't have him. I had Mr. Williams.

B: Do you remember Mr. Lincoln, the Geography teacher?

A: Not really, no. I don't think I had him. But I remember Mr. Connor.

B: Oh yes. We sat together in his Math classes, remember?

A: Of course. We had fun, then.

A: And now it's time for Culture Corner, where we talk about famous writers and artists. Today we are looking at one of the greats of the 20th century. James is here to tell us about the artist Georges Braques. Can you give us some information, James?

B: Well, Braques was born in Argenteuil, near Paris, France. But he lived most of his life in Le Havre, in the north of France.

A: Oh, so he wasn't Spanish like Picasso?

B: No, no.

A: And when was he born?

B: In 1882, and from 1897 to 1899 he went to Art school in Le Havre.

A: OK, and did he meet Picasso at this time?

B: No, he didn't. But he worked very closely with Picasso from 1909 till 1913. And as we all know, the two artists created a new kind of Art, called Cubism.

A: And he spent the rest of his life making cubist works, right?

B: That's right, until he died in 1963.

A: OK, let's take a closer look at his life and work...

A: Hey Tony, what happened to you?

B: I had an accident last night.

A: That's terrible. Are you OK now?

B: Yeah, I suppose so. My head hurts a little.

A: You hurt your head?

B: Yeah, I hit it, but it's not too bad.

A: That's terrible! Tell me what happened. Were you in your dad's car?

B: No, I was in my brother's car, but he's a new driver. Anyway, we were on Bell Road, near our house, when a cat jumped out in front of us.

A: Didn't you see it?

B: We saw it, and we tried not to hit it. But the car swerved and almost hit a motorcycle.

A: Really?

B: Luckily, the man on the motorcycle stopped in time. But we hit a bus stop.

A: Poor you. Were there any people at the bus stop?

B: No, there weren't.

A: What happened then?

B: Well, the man on the motorcycle came and helped.

A: That was nice of him.

B: He took me to the hospital and they checked me out.

A: What about your brother's car?

B: Don't ask. Let's just say, he needs to buy a new one.

A: I see.

Module 9

Now take a look at the information in this table. Can you all see the board? Great. Do you remember the planet we talked about earlier? Look at the numbers referring to size. As you can see, it's smaller than our planet, but it isn't the smallest planet in our solar system. Now, look at the temperatures. The temperatures there are colder than on Earth because it is farther away from the Sun. Now, can anyone tell me why it is also called the Red Planet? Anyone?

9c

A: What's that, Eddie? A monkey?

B: No, it's a baby mountain gorilla.

A: Ah, it's very cute. Is it in a zoo?

B: No, it's in the mountains of central east Africa. That's where mountain gorillas live.

A: They're an endangered species, right?

B: Yes, hunters kill them for their fur, but also for their hands.

A: What? I didn't know that. That's terrible. How many mountain gorillas are there in the wild today?

B: There are only 650, I'm afraid.

A: How awful! What can we do to help them?

B: That's what I'm looking at. On this website, you can adopt a gorilla. I like the idea of that.

A: What else can you do to help?

B: Well, there are lots of great things you can buy, and all the money goes to helping mountain gorillas.

A: Hey, let's get some presents for our friends.

B: That's a great idea. I guess it's better than adopting.

A: I agree. I really like the poster.

B: You know, Richard likes posters. How about getting him that?

A: Good idea.

9d

A: Good afternoon. I would like to ask some questions about your rock climbing school.

B: Certainly, what would you like to know?

A: First of all, do you have a rock climbing wall?

B: Yes, of course. We have two walls inside, but we don't have a climbing wall outside right now.

A: Do you have a wall for beginners? You see, I don't know anything about rock climbing. This is my first time.

B: That's not a problem. We have a beginners' wall, and we have excellent instructors. They are here to help you learn all about rock climbing.

A: What about safety? I mean, it isn't one of the safest sports. It's pretty dangerous when you're up high in the air and everything.

B: Don't worry. You're safe with us. We give you all the safety equipment you need. So, when do you want to start? How about starting lessons tomorrow?

A: Well, I'm kind of busy tomorrow and on the weekend. How about next week? Is that OK? Is an instructor available?

B: Yes, sure. That's fine. Listen, I have an idea. While you're here, how about coming with me? You can talk to Sam. He can give you more information about rock climbing. You see, he's one of the instructors.

A: That's great. I'd like to ask him a few things. Let's go.

Module 10

10b

A: Ahhh, this is the life, huh? Sitting in the sun all day, swimming whenever you like.

B: Oh yeah. Hey, what are we going to do tomorrow?

A: Good question. Would you like to go sightseeing again? The people here at the hotel told me of some places we can visit. There's a nice museum.

B: Yeah, but it's our last day. Don't you want to get some souvenirs for the kids and our friends?

A: You're right. OK, let's go into town in the morning. Then we can go swimming in the afternoon.

B: Sounds good. How about trying some water sports, too?

A: What? On our last day? No way. What if I break a leg or something? How will we travel home? Forget it.

B: OK, OK. I get it. You don't want to.

A: What about dinner? Are we going to have pizza at Ronaldo's? It's the best place around here.

B: Are you kidding? Pizza again? You know, we can't leave this place without trying some of their food.

A: OK, then. Would you like to have dinner at the traditional restaurant in our hotel?

B: I'd love to!

A: What about tonight? Do you want to come fishing with me?

B: What? At night?

A: Yeah, it's the best time to catch fish.

B: No, thanks.

10c

Peter

I go camping every year and I have all the equipment I need: a tent, a sleeping bag, but the most important thing is to be safe. That's why I always make sure I can call somebody when I need to. Here's some advice for your phone: you shouldn't forget to charge it before you leave and you should turn it off for most of the time, so the battery doesn't run out.

Vicky

I went camping last month. I was fine during the day, but at night, it was really dark and very scary. Nobody had an extra flashlight to give me so the next day, I went to a store to buy one. I'm never going to go camping again without one.

Jenny

One thing you need to do on a camping trip is make a fire. It's good for cooking and keeping warm. Always find dry wood to burn, but most important of all, you shouldn't forget to take something with you to light the fire.

Roger

I don't go camping very often so when some friends invited me, I didn't know what to take with me. I took a sleeping bag, some water, but I never thought I'd need sunscreen. I didn't really like the place we went to because there weren't any trees or anything. We went fishing and hiking and had lots of fun, but I got a terrible sunburn. It hurt a lot. You should always remember to take something with you. The sun is very strong nowadays.

A: Hello, Adrian!

B: Colin? What's it like in Crete?

A: It's great. We arrived here two days ago. On the first day we stayed at the hotel all day. It's fantastic and it has a big swimming pool. We were tired so it was a very relaxing day.

B: What about the beaches?

A: Well, we went to a beautiful beach yesterday. The water wasn't very warm but it was nice and I spent the whole day swimming.

B: What else did you do yesterday?

A: My brother went scuba diving, but I didn't like the idea. I don't really like water sports.

B: You should try scuba diving in Crete, though.

A: Anyway, this afternoon we're going hiking. There are some beautiful mountains on the island. And then we're going to have dinner in a small village.

B: What's the food like there? I suppose they have lots of fish.

A: Well, there are lots of different kinds of fish. The fish is OK and the salads are delicious. But do you know what I really like here?

B: What's that?

A: They have lots of delicious cheeses. That was a surprise.

B: What are you going to do tomorrow?

A: Well, we're going to go into town and go shopping in the morning. I want to get some things from Crete for people back home.

B: I hope you're going to get me something, too.

A: Well, I know you hated the T-shirt I got you last year, so this time I'm going to get you a book all about Crete.

B: Sounds interesting.

A: Yes, it looks good and it has some great pictures. Listen, I have to go now. See you when I get back, OK?

B: Yeah, have a great time.

Classroom language

Any questions?
Be quiet, please.
Can you repeat that?
Close your book.
How do you say... in English?
I don't know.
I don't understand.
Listen to the CD.
Look at the board.
Open your book.
Read the text.
Speak in English.
Talk in pairs.
Turn to page...
What does this word mean?
Write a sentence.

Module 1
cover
Hello
What's your name? I'm.../My name's...

1a
last name
Phrases
And you?
Bye
Good afternoon
Good evening
Good morning
Goodbye
Great!
Have a nice day
Hey
Hi
How are you?
How's it going?
I'm fine / Fine
I'm good
I'm OK
I'm very well
Nice to meet you, (too)
Not bad
Not much
See you
See you later
See you tomorrow
Take care
Thank you
Thanks
This is...

What's up?
You too
Titles
Miss
Mr.
Mrs.
Ms.

1b
at (+ place)
call (=give name)
class
classmate
college
cool
friend
here
hospital
no
restaurant
school
so
student
unemployed
yes
Jobs
actor / actress
architect
bus driver
chef
dentist
doctor
electrician
firefighter
nurse
police officer
secretary
teacher
waiter / waitress
Phrases
I'm sorry
It's OK
Really?
Well,...
What about you?
What do you do?

1c
age
avenue
beautiful
best friend
business card
cell (phone)
home
neighbor
new
nice
office
old

over there
photo
road
roommate
send
sick
street
take
today
Numbers
zero - one hundred
Phrases
How old are you? I'm...
   (years old).
I know
Sure
What's your address?
What's your e-mail?
What's your phone number?

1d
but
capital letter
first name
Countries-Nationalities
Argentina - Argentinian/
   Argentine
Australia - Australian
Brazil - Brazilian
Canada - Canadian
China - Chinese
Egypt - Egyptian
France - French
Hungary - Hungarian
Ireland - Irish
Italy - Italian
Mexico - Mexican
Peru - Peruvian
Poland - Polish
Russia - Russian
Spain - Spanish
the U.K. - British
the U.S.A. - American
Turkey - Turkish
Phrases
How do you spell...?
I live in...
Where are you from? I'm
   from...

Module 2
cover
backpack
folder
notebook
pen
pencil
Colors
black
blue

brown
green
orange
pink
purple
red
white
yellow
Phrases
What color is/are...?
What's your favorite...?

2a
big
boy
child - children
girl
kid
man
married
middle name
only
single
small
woman
Family
baby
brother
dad
daughter
father
grandfather
grandmother
grandparents
husband
mom
mother
parents
sister
son
wife
Phrases
Do you have any brothers
   or sisters?
I'm an only child
What's your name again?
Who...?
Yeah

2b
about (=around)
all the time
awesome
cheap
day and night
expensive
game
lots of
movie
music

of course
picture
song
terrible
train (n.)
work (n.)

Words/Phrases related to technology
camera
CD
DVD
gadget
headphones
Internet
keyboard
laptop
MP4 player
PC (personal computer)
screen
smartphone
tablet
USB memory stick

Phrases
I have it with me
I like...
I love...
I think...

2c
bag
both
brush
car
chewing gum
dictionary
ID card
in
keys
mad
magazine
outside
sunglasses
ticket
tissues
umbrella
wallet
watch (n.)

Phrases
What are these/those?
What's this/that?
Whose...?
You're right

2d
also
other
thing

Words/Phrases related to appearance
blond

chubby
dark
eyes
good-looking
gray
hair
handsome
in his/her 20s/30s...
long
medium-height
medium-length
middle-aged
overweight
short
slim
tall
young

Module 3
cover
weekday
weekend

Days of the week
Monday
Tuesday
Wednesday
Thursday
Friday
Saturday
Sunday

3a
all
chocolate
coffee
croissant
different
early
finish
for
library
make
start
store
with

Words/Phrases related to time
a.m.
after
at
every day
from... to...
midnight
noon
o'clock
p.m.
then
What time is it? It's...

Daily routines
get home

get up
go to bed
go to work/school
have a class
have breakfast/lunch/dinner
study
take a shower
watch TV
work (v.)

3b
actually
at all
ball
boring
come
fun
hate
need
park
present (n.)
pretty (adv.)
really (adv.)
running shoes
together
very much

Sports
do gymnastics
do track and field
go bowling
go cycling
go running
go swimming
play baseball
play basketball
play ping-pong
play soccer
play tennis
play volleyball

Phrases
Excuse me...
Let's...
That's a good idea
You see...

3c
a day
a lot of
alone
be good at + noun
before
check (v.)
colleague
easy
female
find
hard
hour
just
male

problem
same
sell
serious
team
try

Spare-time activities
go for coffee
go shopping
go to a game
go to the gym
go to the movies
hang out with friends
listen to music
play video games
read the newspaper

Phrases
In my spare time...
When...?

3d
channel
exercise (v.)
interest
run
stay home
treadmill
TV guide

TV shows
documentary
game show
sitcom
soap opera
sports
talent show
talk show
the news
the weather

Phrases
Me too.
What kind of TV shows...?
What time is it on?
What's on?
When...

Module 4
cover
Rooms of a house
bathroom
bedroom
kitchen
living room

Household items
air conditioner (AC)
chair
lamp
mirror
table

4a

because
buy
can't stand
clean (adj.)
dirty
dishwasher
floor (of a room)
furniture
help (v.)
late
messy
minute
tell
want to
yard

Chores

clean
cook
do housework
do the laundry
do/wash the dishes
go grocery shopping
mow the lawn
take out the trash
vacuum
wash the car

Adverbs of frequency

always
usually
often
sometimes
never

Phrase

Check it out

4b

clock
door
rug
sink
sit down
trash can
wall
window

Furniture

armchair
bed
bookcase
coffee table
couch
desk

Appliances

oven
refrigerator

stove
washing machine

Prepositions of place

behind
in
in front of
next to
on
under

Phrases

Don't mention it
Let me help you
Maybe...
Perhaps...
Watch out

4c

extra
furnished
large
mind (v.)
modern
now
rent (v.)

**Parts of a house/
apartment**

backyard
balcony
closet
downstairs
elevator
front yard
garage
stairs
upstairs

Phrases

How many...?
Not really
That sounds nice

4d

city
cozy
double bed
fantastic
floor (of a building)
microwave
single bed
view

Ordinals

first
second
third, etc.

Phrases

What floor do you live on?
  On the...
Where exactly?

Module 5
5a

bicycle lane
businesswoman
downtown
elementary school
far
fast
get around
give sb. a ride
money
near
neighborhood
people
public transportation
race
radio
right now
station
swim
think
town
traffic
use
walk

Modes of transportation

drive a car
ride a bike
ride a motorcycle
take a cab/taxi
take the bus
take the subway

Phrase

How do you get to...?

5b

a ten-minute walk
know one's way around
map
stop
traffic lights
wait

Places in a city

airport
bank
coffee shop
gas station
hotel
movie theater
parking lot
police station
shopping mall
supermarket

Prepositions of place

across from
between

Directions

Go down...
Go straight
How can/do I get to...?

It's on your left/right
Turn left/right at the...

Phrases

Don't worry
It takes...
No problem

5c

bench
bottle
bring
call (=phone)
can (n.)
clean up
clothes
energy
environment
etc.
faucet
fence
give
information
lights
organize
paint
pick up (trash)
plant (v.)
poster
protect
put
put up (a fence)
recycle
recycling bin
save
throw away
tree
turn off
volunteer (n.)
water
website

Phrases

I (don't) think so
I'm not sure about that

5d

beach
building
excellent
famous
fish
forget
go for a walk
history
important
learn
like (prep.)
over (=more than)
painting
play (n.)
popular

remember
scooter
tourist
tram
visit
wild animal
Sights
aquarium
castle
market
museum
stadium
theater
zoo
Phrases
Don't miss...
The best way to see...

Module 6
cover
Food
pizza
salad
sandwich
soup
tomato

6a
all kinds of
delicious
eat
especially
even
garden
good for you
however
meal
plant (n.)
vegetarian
Food and drink
apple
banana
beef
bread
carrot
cheese
chicken
cucumber
dairy products
egg
fruit
juice
lamb
lettuce
meat
milk
onion
orange
pasta
pineapple

potato
rice
snack
steak
strawberry
vegetable
yogurt

6b
be ready
change
customer
dessert
drink (v.)
look good
order (v.)
without
Food and drink
apple pie
cake
cappuccino
chicken nuggets
cinnamon
(French) fries
ice cream
ketchup
mayonnaise
mushroom
mustard
onion rings
pepper
salt
soda
sugar
tacos
tea
tuna
vanilla
Phrases
Anything else?
Anything to drink?
Are you ready to order?
Certainly.
I'd like...
I'm afraid...
Is that all?
That's all.
Would you like to order?
Would you like... with that?

6c
answer (v.)
appointment
ask
busy
eating habits
group
healthy
hungry
junk food

survey
thirsty
Food and drink
cheesecake
(potato) chips
chocolate bar
cookie
hot chocolate
lemon
sauce
Phrases denoting quantity
a bag of
a bar of
a bottle of
a box of
a can of
a cup of
a glass of
a slice of
Phrases
All right.
I guess

6d
a type of
during
fried
include
not many
skip
traditional
Food and drink
baked potato
beans
butter
cereal
donut
jam
milkshake
noodles
omelet
pancakes
syrup
toast
waffles

Module 7
cover
chat on the Net
check e-mail
download information/
  songs/movies
online
surf the Net

7a
call back
flower
graduation

instant messaging
make a phone call
send a text message
sir
skype (n.+v.)
spring
talk on the phone
use a social media site
Phrases
Can I leave a message?
Hold on
How may I help you?
I can't talk right now
I'm..., by the way.
I'm (just) kidding
Is... there?
Listen,...
Yep

7b
antivirus software
area
assignment
battery
be stuck
button
charge (v.)
enter password
first thing in the morning
happen
have trouble with
install
leave
look for
nothing
paper
press
print
printer
program
show (v.)
someone
something
technician
turn on/off
username
Phrases
Can I/you give you/me a
  hand?
Can you help me?
I don't know how to...
Need any help?
Thank you so much
Thanks anyway
That's very kind of you.
What can I do for you?
You're welcome

7c
all over the world

almost
and so on
arrow
confusing
difficult
for example
hand
instead of
lucky
point (v.)
quiz
simple
speaker (person)
technology
useful
user
Computer language
click (v.)
copy
cut
delete
document
file
key
mouse
paste
save
shortcut
Phrase
Which...?

7d
annoying
concert
decide
exam
for a while
have a good time
inside
loud
take a break
tonight
Phrases related to weather
It's cloudy
It's cold
It's hot
It's raining
It's snowing
It's sunny
It's warm
It's windy
What's the weather like?
Phrases
Anyway,...

Dear...
How about...?
How's life?
I hope you're...
That sounds like fun
That's all for now
Write back soon
Yours,...

Module 8
cover
memory
vacation

8a
ago
at least
enjoy
for ages
hat
horrible
last night, etc.
little
piece
purse
share
the other side
the whole time
ugly
wear
yesterday

8b
artist
back then
become
century
choose
computer programmer
cousin
graduate
high school
major in
teach
thousand
Subjects
Art
Biology
Chemistry
English Literature
Geography
Gym
History
IT (Information Technology)
Mathematics (Math)
Physics
Phrases
It's a small world
What a surprise!
Why...?

You look familiar

8c
act (v.)
at the age of
be born
begin
classic
dance
dancer
die
direct
director
explore
explorer
invent
inventor
novel
painter
poem
poet
publish
sing
singer
still
story
successful
village
writer

8d
be closed
break (v.)
bus stop
cat
crash (into)
day off
fall (off)
feel
go wrong
happy
have an accident
hit
hurt (v.)
in the end
jump
luckily
sad
sidewalk
wake up
Parts of the body
arm
ear
finger
foot - feet
head
knee
leg
mouth
nose

tooth - teeth
Phrases
Did you break anything?
How awful!
How unlucky!
I'm sorry to hear that
Oh no! That's terrible!
Poor you
What a day!
What's wrong?

Module 9
cover
billion
extreme
million

9a
careful
casual
extra small/large
follow
formal
in the beginning
salesperson
Clothes and accessories
baseball cap
dress
jacket
jeans
pants
shirt
shorts
skirt
suit
sweater
tie
T-shirt
Footwear
boots
shoes
sneakers
Money
cents
dollar
euro
pence
pound
Phrases
How much is it / are they?
I wear a size...
I'll take it/them.
What do you think of...?
What size do you wear?

9b
astronomy
bright
close (adj.)
correct (adj.)

discover
Earth
fit (v.)
galaxy
last (v.)
mile
moon
move
next
object
planet
reach
science
sky
solar system
star
sun
telescope
temperature
wrong

9c
adopt
as a result
climb
destroy
donate
endangered species
event
farm animal
farmer
fur
habitat
high
hunter
in the wild
interesting
join
keep
kill
local people
lonely
mountain
organization
reason
shy
snow (n.)
stuffed animal
take a picture
Animals
camel
deer
dolphin
elephant
goat
gorilla
leopard
lion
panda
sheep

snake
tiger
Phrases
I agree
I don't agree

9d
a little
colorful
dangerous
deep
equipment
exciting
instructor
safe
scared
scary
Extreme sports
hang gliding
mountain biking
rock climbing
sailing
scuba diving
skydiving
surfing
Phrases
Guess what!
No way

Module 10
cover
Kinds of vacation
backpacking
by a beach
camping
cruise
sightseeing tour
skiing

10a
airplane
arrive
flight
hockey
travel
Seasons
spring
summer
fall
winter
Months
January
February
March
April
May
June
July
August
September

October
November
December
Phrase
What's the date today?

10b
be/get bored
complain
invitation
invite
kind of (=pretty)
tired
Geographical features
forest
island
lake
ocean
river
sea
Vacation activities
buy postcards
buy souvenirs
do water sports
go fishing
go hiking
go sightseeing
taste local food
Phrases
I have other plans
Maybe some other time
See you in a while
Thanks for inviting me
Why not?

10c
abroad
advice
campfire
campground
credit card
culture
definitely
find out
first-aid kit
flashlight
go on a trip
matches
necessary
passport
phrasebook
relaxing
sleep (v.)
sleeping bag
strong
such as
suitcase
sunscreen
swimsuit
tent

the first time
traveler
visa
worried
Phrases
How long...?
I believe...
Make sure...

10d
active
amazing
barbecue
boat
catch (fish)
comfortable
court
excited
huge
jealous
lose
nature
perfect
prefer
relax
spend (time)
sunset
swimming pool
whale shark
win

Pioneer Beginners
American edition
Student's Book
H. Q. Mitchell - Marileni Malkogianni

Published by: **MM Publications**
www.mmpublications.com
info@mmpublications.com

Offices
UK China Cyprus Greece Korea Poland Turkey USA
Associated companies and representatives throughout the world.

Copyright © 2013 MM Publications

Produced in the EU

ISBN978-4-7647-4157-7

C1903007042-15735